MAPPING SOCIAL GAZE

On Global Governance

MAPPING SOCIAL GAZE

On Global Governance

Series Editor
Badri Narayan

Editor
Bhaskar Majumder

G.B. Pant Memorial Lectures Series
Part-II

Vani Book Company
An imprint of Vani Prakashan Group

Vani Book Company
An imprint of Vani Prakashan Group

Head Office

4695, 21-A, Daryaganj, New Delhi 110 002, India
Phone +91 11 23273167 Fax : +91 11 23275710

Registered Bookstores and Offices

Ashok Rajpath, Patna 800 004, Bihar
Coffee House Campus, Mahatma Gandhi Marg, Allahabad 211 001, Uttar Pradesh
Mahatma Gandhi International Hindi University, Wardha 442 001, Maharashtra
Sultania Road, Moti Park, Bhopal 462 001, Madhya Pradesh
Goripur Taliya Para, 313, R.B.C. Road 24- Parganas (North) Kolkata 743 166, West Bengal

www.vaniprakashan.com
marketing@vaniprakashan.in
sales@vaniprakashan.in

Mapping Social Gaze : On Global Governance
Series Editor : Badri Narayan
Editor : Bhaskar Majumder

ISBN : 978-93-5518-059-9
Social Science

First Edition 2022

Price : ₹ 399

Printed and bound in India at R. Tek Offset Printers, Delhi-110 032

Vani Prakashan's signature motif is created by Artist Maqbool Fida Husain

Preface

This book is a collection of lectures delivered by eminent scholars invited every year on the occasion of the Foundation Day of the G. B. Pant Social Science Institute, Prayagraj (formerly Allahabad. I am extremely privileged to have been invited by the Director of the Institute, Prof. Badri Narayan, to be Editor of this prestigious volume.

My task was simple. I had only to arrange the articles as they were. After perusing the essays, my task was to add an Introduction which I have tried my best to do, but I feel I stand nowhere close to the scholarly articles in this volume.

This book is the second in the series *Social Gaze*' which the Institute launched very recently. I am sure this book will be an important addition to that series. I am thankful for the immense support from the staff of the Institute in completing this manuscript. In case any shortcoming is noticed in the book, I apologize for that.

–*Bhaskar Majumder*
Prayagraj

Introduction

Globalization is not something new in the post-Second World War world economy; however, the forms and forces of globalization might not have moved in a linear fashion throughout the path of recorded history (Gomes, 2003: 301-302). Globalization has been in existence since the beginning of civilization when human beings settled down and began producing and exchanging goods. Since historical times there has been free movement of people for trade and knowledge. History is replete with examples of kings, soldiers and historians who moved out from their roots and recorded their travel-related experiences. The borders being open, people could move more easily than now. For example, Rome was an 'epitome' of the whole world – 'city-as-world', where people from every corner of the world settled. Between 220 BC and 167 BC the Romans had succeeded in bringing under their rule almost the whole of the countries around the Mediterranean including Europe, North Africa and West Asia. 'By the first century A.D., Rome had extensive trade links with India, Malaysia and even China…' that showed steady movement of goods (Robertson & Inglis, 2006:13-16).

The history of European expansionism radically changed the earlier mode of global links; for example, as manifest in Roman imperialism, in scale, longevity and the type of overseas domination. The new mode relied on 'systematic interventions of states' aimed at establishing and maintaining rules by its sovereign power over the subordinate and alien people (Jones &Philips, 2006: 29, 39-40). Historically speaking, 'the world of the late 1800s and early 1900s was more tightly integrated through trade than today. There was certainly a greater movement of people. Cotton was introduced to world trade from India as early as 600 BC, and followed the trade routes to Syria, Cyprus, Sicily, Tunisia, Morocco, and Spain and eventually to the Nile Valley. India was probably the world's largest exporter from 1500 to 1700 A.D. Islamic trade routes brought paper-making art from China to Europe and Greek medicine back into a Europe that had lost it during the dark ages…' (Moore, 2003: 24). The half a century preceding the First World War showed rapid international integration, with trade flows representing a very high share of GDP in the UK, the Netherlands, and Japan (Petit & Soete, 1999:166). By the mid-nineteenth century, it came to be realized that the controllers of capital would nestle everywhere, settle everywhere, and establish connections everywhere (Marx &

Engels, 1977: 46). Not only capital but also commodities and people moved on a large scale during the half century before the First World War. Between 1870 and 1914, around 36 million people crossed the Atlantic from Europe, two-thirds of them to the United States alone. A record 1.28 million immigrants poured into the United States in 1907. The workers, understood as unskilled today, moved freely with minimum government regulation without any need for passports and in the early phase of the exodus, with the aid of government subsidies (like assisted passages) (Gomes, 2003:304). Passport controls were introduced in Europe only after the First World War to prevent the enemy from entering national territory and to control ethnic composition of population-cum-workforce. Later the Great Depression (1929-1933) discouraged migration in view of rising unemployment in the capitalist world (Nayyar, 2002a:146).

However, the movement of people across regions not necessarily confined to sovereign countries perhaps did not show a system since a system evolves through systematic modes of operation by conscious participants in an interdependent frame. The system that we talk about today had its roots in the European system. The European system evolved in order to showcase the advances of European countries in technology and trade, which gave birth to the capitalist system. The roots of the capitalist system was located in the late fifteenth century Europe but the capitalist system expanded in space over time to cover the entire globe by the late nineteenth century (Wallerstein, 1987:19). This form of globalization was led by the UK as the dominant superpower in the late nineteenth century and is a prominent example of colonial-political type of territorial extension. France, the Netherlands and Portugal were some of the other countries that followed this path.

Before the First World War, because of pre-1914 advances in transport technology, the trade of some countries with the outside world formed a significant proportion of the GDP. However, the post-Second World War-specific globalization is characterized by advanced technology that makes the movement of physical objects, of money-capital and of ideas, much easier and cheaper than in the past and at a speed that the governments in national economies find difficult to control. The present form of economic globalization has created a 'borderless world' by the establishment and functioning of transnational networks centered on production-trade-finance, first for economic benefits and subsequently for political mileage and military conquest. This form of globalization is being led by the US, the most powerful nation in the world today, with the help of the other Developed Market Economies (DMEs) of the world.

The revolutionary developments in the field of electronics or internet in the late twentieth century made information global and converted the national economies into globalized economies (Beedham, 1999:38). The framework is financed by invisible unregulated (electronically regulated) exchanges of money, credit and equities. In fact, 'the degree of capital mobility of late 20th century globalization in both currency markets and in bonds, equity, short-term credit and other financial instruments is of unprecedented nature in history. Second, in early twentieth century globalization, there were no global financial or political institutions aimed at stabilizing the world economy, financing development, setting global rules for international trade in goods and services (the World Trade Organization), and provide a political and diplomatic forum to settle disputes among states and address a host of other global issues such as the United Nations. Third, there was a change in the leadership in the two waves of globalization (www.sice.oas.org, May 7th, 2004).

Post-Second World War globalization corresponded to a mature stage of capitalist industrialization where new global markets started emerging. These were the markets in banking, insurance, and services. Financial institutions, such as the Multinational Banks (MNBs), started following the new extra-national actors, that is, the Transnational Corporations (TNCs). The post-Second World War globalization was new in terms of its shift from product-specific comparative cost-linked social division of labour to global division of labour. The latter accommodated both labour-intensive and capital-intensive processes in different locations (countries) to produce a single product. The development of technology, increasingly controlled by the TNCs, made this 'two techniques-two spaces-one product' a success. The TNCs located production activities in different countries according to their master strategy and integrated them through intra-firm (and/or inter-firm) networks of trade (UNCTAD, 1997: 164). The global division of labour is market-centered and not product-centered. Though camouflaged by an omnipotent market, the outcomes of globalization were politically pre-fixed; they were not pre-determined by some invisible hand of international market forces (Peck & Yeung, 2003: 164). In fact, pure markets do not exist, what we understand as markets are shaped by different configurations of legal frameworks, social conventions, power relations, and institutional forces.

The post-Second World War globalization was also new by constitution of policy coordination groups and their domination in shaping global economic phenomena. These groups often overshadowed the national priorities of countries that are not members of these groups. The post-Second World War globalization also framed a new legal system where world institutions like the World Bank, International Monetary Fund, and WTO executed the rules for governance of the countries. Globalization of the second half of the twentieth century was, thus, circumscribed by the laws framed by the developed market economies. One of the reasons for the setting up of global policy institutions was the occurrence of major economic crises, particularly in the third world countries, since the 1970s. These included debt crises of the 1980s, the Mexican crises of 1994, and the Asian financial crises of 1997 (www.sice.oas.org, May 7, 2004). The increasingly inter-dependent financial and trade flows during the second phase had also been joined by and come into conflict with the global trend towards greater transparency, democratization and instantaneous dissemination of ideas, accelerated by the economic-electronic freedom as well as anarchy of the internet (Moore, 2003: 16). Thus, globalization brought about questions centered on how to manage it, that is, its governance.

Globalization downsized nation states. It produced its own economic geography with its decision-making centres in the US and the UK, its planned shifting frontiers of extension and mediation such as South Africa, Eastern Europe, Japan and Latin America, and its sites of active contestation and resistance like in many of the Third World countries. Indeed, even if they were unequal partners, nation states were the actors in the globalization project. In the 1990s, the autonomy of the state from the Third World, excepting perhaps a few, is much reduced at least in economic affairs. There are catalysts and agencies in both collaboration with and conflict against the nation states. Governments now share the stage with the corporate world and civil society. The institutions and rules for governance of the world economy are, therefore, less compatible with the changed reality now (Nayyar, 2002b: 7).

Post-Second World War, globalization can be seen as being divided into two phases, depending on the strategy and execution of measures taken by the dominant countries. The first phase was the phase of 'intensive globalization' characterized by selection of a few close countries by the dominant countries to be the trade-centers for the latter. The second one was the phase of 'extensive globalization' characterized by a strategy of the dominant countries to extend their production possibilities via encompassing large economies in the developing world to take advantage of the large potential markets of the latter using the transnational corporations at the command of the former.

Intensive Globalization

The strategy followed during the post-Second World War period was 'intensive' globalization. This strategy was evidenced when some of the initially small economies either established links with the DMEs or continued their colonially established linkages. The four first-tier Newly Industrialized Countries (NICs), namely, Hong Kong, Singapore, Taiwan, and South Korea are examples of some of these small economies. All these economies became 'newly industrialized' by exercise of the strategy of export-led industrialization, accompanied by inflow of capital invested through the TNCs that originate from the DMEs (Chew & Denmark, 1996: 7). The export-based dependent industrialization of the NICs was also beneficial for the DMEs since they were able to shift their capital to these NICs, relocate their production space, and export the surplus produced in the host NICs. The internal market of these NICs being very small, the strategy served mutual interest. The NICs promoted their exports while the DMEs through the TNCs located in the NICs, expanded their production space by export of capital. Thus, these small economies came to absorb the surplus capital of the DMEs by offering space for investment. This helped the DMEs to extend their production space and re-export the surplus product. However, these small economies could serve only a limited purpose of the DMEs. Consequently, second-tier NICs came to serve the DMEs. These were the ASEAN countries in the (Association of South East Asian Nations) which included Indonesia, Malaysia, the Philippines, and Thailand. These economies were bigger in size than the first-tier NICs. The emergence of these countries gave the DMEs a better chance not only to solve the realization problem, but also to utilize more resources owned by these relatively larger economies.

The first-tier Newly Industrialized Countries (NICs), which were the export-dependent small economies, developed a peculiar economic structure by the mid-1990s. Of these NICs, the first two were 'city states', or the 'trading stations for the Imperial Power'. Originally Hong Kong became a colony by conquest, taken from China following the Treaty of Nanking, 1842, and the Convention of Peking, 1960. Its function was to serve as a naval base from which the China coast could be policed. Hong Kong developed first into a major commercial center, which after 1950 became a big industrial city-state (Darwin, 1988: 310). Hong Kong was transferred from the UK to China on July 1, 1997. The population of Hong Kong happens to be 100 per cent Chinese. Singapore separated herself from Malaysia, became independent in 1965 and soon became dependent on the TNCs for entrepreneurship and technology (Lee, 1997: 58-61, 68). In the eighteenth and early nineteenth centuries, the island of Singapore came under British possession to be used as her 'trading station'. By exercise of political authority, Singapore came within what may be called the 'British Malaya', a federation-type network (Darwin, 1988: 106-107). Up to the 1950s, Singapore worked as a 'city-state', a 'trading-station' as well as a 'client state' for the British. During the 1980s, foreign firms commanded almost the whole of the gross sales within Singapore and most of her exports (Rasiah, 1994: 209). The domination of foreign capital converted the 'city-state' into a 'transnational city state'. By the 1980s, however, Singapore had shown its exhaustion to the imperial system.

The stories of Taiwan and Korea were different from those of Hong Kong and Singapore. Both Korea and Taiwan were colonies of Japan. Taiwan had a narrow home market as well as a foreign exchange constraint, which induced the Government of Taiwan to pursue an oppressive export-oriented policy in the late 1950s. For easy export promotion, the government invited foreign investments into the manufacturing sector (Hung, 1996: 153). Economic growth in Korea did not depend on the domestic market, but became increasingly dependent on exports, particularly to the US consumer market. An important factor facilitating the Export-Oriented Industrialization (EOI) strategy adopted by the NICs was their access to the major markets of the DMEs, particularly Japan, and the US. In other words, the NIC-type development strategy had two long-term external bases, namely, the US and Japan. Japan provided technology, capital goods, and trading companies for these NICs to launch their export-led growth; the US provided a massive consumer market. The other base for the export success of these NICs was 'command capitalism', whereby the condition of the working class was kept to the minimum level (Burbach, 1997: 89). In fact, these NICs depended for their success on their possible access to the markets of the US and Japan on the one hand, and the operation of 'command capitalism' on the other. During the 1950s, Japan had been working hard to look for overseas bases where labour would be cheaper than what it was in the domestic market. In the struggle against communism, the non-communist countries nearest to Japan were her earliest colonies, namely, Korea and Taiwan. Japan promoted these two countries and by the same process extended her own production bases.

The strategy of intensive globalization however, had several contradictions, which led to it gradually being rejected. The DMEs that were guided by their logic of protecting themselves against the steady entry of the 'small market' 'close' economies also obstructed the aggressive entry of the NICs. For example, the US efforts to protect its own markets were directed not only against Japan but also against the four first-tier NICs. In addition, neither Western Europe nor Japan was willing to open their markets to absorb the proportion of goods that were going to the US (Burbach, 1997: 89). The DMEs resisted the uninterrupted success of the TWCs through exports both by protecting home firms operating at home and by imposing export restrictions on TWC firms operating in the TWCs. The trade strategies that could be followed by the NICs were ruled out for the TWCs. After the Plaza Accord of1985, the competitiveness of Korean exports improved. However, the Korean exports caused trade frictions in various overseas markets, including the United States and countries in Europe. In this phase, Korea had to abandon its export promotion policy, which had continued for about three decades (Okuda, 1997: 360).

While the US and the International Financial Institutions (IFIs) have already cited the NICs as examples of export-led growth, the US understood the forces that might lead to exhaustion of market-expansion in the NICs. The magnitude and the rate of growth of GNP are the basic determinants for an economy's participation in trade. Korea had been cited as a successful example of 'trickle down' and stable economic growth, but the dependency aspect of this growth is often missing. Japan and the US were the main protectors of Korea. Up to the mid-1960s the share of foreign savings in Korea's investment came mainly from the US, while Japan took the lead from the early 1970s. Dependence for investment on a few DMEs itself showed the structural weakness of a particular country in executing the development strategy, particularly if that country happened to be small.

The same type of story can be told about the Association of South East Asian Nations (ASEAN). The ASEAN was in effect an expansion and supersession of the Association of South East Asia (ASEA) established by Malaya, the Philippines, and Thailand in July 1961, and dissolved on 29 August, 1967. The ASEAN revived again in the late 1960s with Indonesia's membership in it, and this revival was significant since Indonesia alone had half of the total population of countries in the ASEAN. The ASEAN also depended heavily on the US and Japan for its trade. Thus, it was mainly the DMEs who constituted the market for ASEAN tradable products.

Indonesia, the Philippines, and Thailand, as the major members in the ASEAN, who were among the second-tier NICs, had much larger endowments of natural resources and much larger population size relative to the four first-tier East Asian NICs. These NICs in the second tier had a potentially larger pool of skilled labour and domestic demand than the four tigers. Also, FDI inflows from the US, the EU, and Japan in the economies in ASEAN, gave scope for business cooperation in ASEAN. These also connected export markets in East and South East Asia and in the rest of the world. Particularly, Japan played a vital role as a source of technology and of foreign direct investment for both the first-tier and the second-tier NICs. The appreciation of the yen relative to the US dollar after the Plaza Accord of 1985 led the Japanese investors to shift capital from Japan to the second-tier NICs (Bagchi, 1998: 1026, 1029). Naturally, these second-tier NICs experienced growth rates during the 1990s even more than that of Japan. The point to be emphasized here is that these NICs expanded in a dependent manner (Aseniero, 1996: 189). One of the consequences was that the flow of foreign investments, directed mainly by market forces, led to destabilizing effects on these economies. In general, the imbalances in regional integration, the dependence of these economies on borrowing from the DMEs, and the falling terms of trade for products of these economies led to the 1997 'currency crisis' or 'crisis of destabilization' for the ASEAN. The crux of the crisis was financial. In Indonesia, the Republic of Korea, Malaysia, the Philippines, and Thailand, the real effective exchange rates depreciated between 30.0 and 60.0 per cent between June 1997 and January 1998. While Thailand and Malaysia could maintain balance in exchange rate vis-à-vis the US dollar, the Philippines and Indonesia experienced marginal devaluation (ADB, Asian Development Outlook, several issues; *IMF, International Financial Statistics*, various issues).

The downward spiral of currency depreciation and stock market decline that started in mid-1997 undermined the viability of heavily indebted financial institutions and corporations, drying up liquidity and freezing investment and even production. Together with high interest rates throughout the region to shore up exchange rates, there began a series of bankruptcies of heavily indebted corporations, which further weakened the local financial institutions (UN, Department of Economic and Social Affairs, 1998: 40-41). The economies could not rely on domestic demand because of their long-term dependence on the DMEs for trade, technology and finance. At the end of 1997, the high interest rates accompanied by heavy corporate debt burdens led to contraction of investment in all these economies, namely, Indonesia, Thailand, and the Republic of Korea. Parallel to this, excepting Korea, the economies of Indonesia, Malaysia, and Thailand could not promote exports, although they tried with respect to currency depreciation. The major impediment to responding to the price incentive from the lower exchange rate had been the lack, because of the financial crisis, of domestic working capital and external credit for import of necessary inputs. In addition, the increase in the cost of imported inputs and the concurrent depreciation in competing countries in the region have partly offset the favourable price effect of the currency depreciation. Moreover, the economic slowdown in Japan, a major market for East Asian exports, dampened export demand (UN, Department of Economic and Social Affairs, 1998: 42).

Even if the economic fundamentals are not too weak, the contradiction in this process of dependent expansion is that once it starts, it generates surplus products and capital that need to be realized. These need expanding the commodity market to absorb the surplus products and expanding the credit market to absorb capital. The economic space too needs expansion for realization of expanding capital. The physical space that initially gets converted into capital-realizing economic space fails ultimately to retain capital within the physical territory. The strategy of intensive globalization hence faced its limit, imposed by the requirements of both expanding commodity and credit markets. The small economies, as the space for intensive globalization, ceased to remain attractive because the rate of growth of capital exceeds the rate at which economic space grows for further realization of capital. Since capital converts physical space into an economic space, the physical-economic space bounded by the nation-state cannot confine capital to its own territory once capital is allowed to expand. Thus, the strategy of intensive globalization was replaced by the strategy of extensive globalization.

Extensive Globalization

Extensive globalization was the strategy of the countries of G-7 led by the US to extend their production boundary via penetration into the potential markets of large economies in the developing world with the help of the Transnational Corporations (TNCs) at their command. Extensive globalization was the context that showed the economic compulsions of the Big Power (G-7) and the scope for Large Economies (Majumder, 1997: 298-300; Majumder, 1998:43).

The end of the Second World War made it necessary for countries to minimize economic costs by formation of groups of countries of similar interests. For example, in 1947 the United States initiated the Marshall Plan for the economic recovery of Europe. It insisted that the European countries should cooperate in the allocation of US funds. The Organization for European Economic Cooperation (OEEC) was established for this purpose. In 1960, the OEEC became the Organization for Economic Cooperation and Development (OECD). Initially the OECD had the United States and Canada as members. Eventually most of the western industrialized countries joined it (Brandt, 1980: 37). The OECD countries, because of their high per capita income and high national income, were the main destinations of exports from the export-oriented TWCs. OECD countries as the export destinations for the TWCs was also because of a similar exportable product structure of the TWCs who would be internally competing unless they aimed at the countries with a different product structure. Of all the goods exported to the DMEs by the TWCs, the share of manufactured goods increased over time. This increasing share in exports was, however, concentrated to a few TWCs. The general nature of dependence of the TWCs on the DMEs for importing capital goods remained unchanged (World Bank, 1998, WDI: 323). The access of countries to foreign direct investment also remained concentrated.

Following the disintegration of the USSR and the reunification of Germany, both of which took place in 1989, the US faced two problems. The first was managing the internal distribution of power among countries within the First World, and the second was controlling the Third World. Historically, the extraction of resources in the Third World has been dominated by the network of transnational corporations, which provided capital, technology and marketing facilities, and shouldered the exploration risk themselves. Immediately after the Second World War, the newly born TWCs had little knowledge about the far-reaching implications of their agreements with the TNCs exploiting the mineral and other natural resources of their economies. By implication, these TWCs had little idea about the costs and benefits from extraction of the resources they were endowed with. Consequently they were the victims of excess costs over benefits. Naturally, their own negotiating position vis-à-vis an exploration company originating from any DME was extremely weak (Brandt, 1980: 155). It was only after the exercise of power by OPEC through manifold increase in oil price in 1973 that the TWCs were apparently empowered vis-à-vis the DMEs. The declaration of New International Economic Order (NIEO) in the UN in 1974 also brought this pattern of exploration and investment on the brink of breaking down.

This situation compelled the US to initiate measures to contain the Third World pressure, accommodate close dependents and allies, and contain challenges from within. While by the end of the nineteenth century, Britain had realized the advancement of Germany and the US in terms of industrial output and productivity (Gamble, 1990: 74), by the end of the twentieth century, the US had become aware of the potentiality of Japan and a united Germany in the changed world. Japan of early twenty-first century, however, was unwilling or unable to play a role in the world proportionate to its economic size.

In the globalized world, the large emerging market economies from the Third World saw themselves as potential beneficiaries by being in the list of investment by the TNCs. The potential challengers of the leader (US) within G-7 in the same process got the opportunities for entry into the markets of the TWCs, which suit them (Majumder, 1998: 52-53). Extensive globalization thus worked as a strategy for the world leaders. However, at the level of execution, this strategy might face obstructions because of differences between the major TWCs and the dominant DMEs. Hence, the change from intensive to extensive globalization required governance by global policy institutions.

Global Governance: Concept and Principles

'Governance is the sum of many ways individuals and institutions, public and private, manage their common affairs. It is a continuing process through which conflicting or diverse interests may be accommodated and co-operative action may be taken. It includes formal institutions and regimes empowered to enforce compliance, as well as informal arrangements that people and institutions either have agreed to or perceive to be in their interest' (The Commission on Global Governance, 1995: 2).

Global Governance is not a government but a framework of minimum rules necessary to tackle global problems, guaranteed by a set of institutions including both international organizations and national governments. Global Governance aims at accepting objectives and implementing them at the global/regional level. The foundation for global governance is the belief that the world is now ready to accept a "global civic ethic" based on a set of core values aimed at uniting people of all cultural, political, religious, or ideological backgrounds. This belief is reinforced by the idea that governance should carry with it democracy at all levels and ultimately be enforceable by law. The objectives of global governance may be economic-financial stability in the economic domain and ensuring diplomatic stability in the political domain. Governance looks into countries' external relations vis-à-vis other countries, and also sometimes internal relations within a particular country if that affect global stability. Governance may be taken to imply the way in which decisions and policies are prepared and executed; that is, it focuses on the process that connects the catalysts. In the presence of a global economy and simultaneously in the absence of a global polity, the ability to govern the market may be difficult, because market is an abstraction, or a context of rules formed/framed by institutions. In this sense market reflects an institution (Griffin, 2003: 790).

The purpose of Global Governance centers on regulation of state and state power, regulation over transnational corporations and regulation over markets. The White Paper of the European Commission 2001 identified the principles of 'good governance' as one which should include openness, participation, accountability, effectiveness and coherence (Commission of the European Communities, 2001: 10).

Participation of all the stake holders throughout the policy chain – from conception to implementation -- is a prerequisite of good governance. However, participation alone cannot ensure effective governance. Participation of a few actors of civil society and absence of proper guidelines for effective participation of all the stake holders may lead to 'oligarchist' governance and not a democratic one. Participatory governance acknowledges that there is a multiplicity of actors who hold interests, rights and competencies in public choice and public policy; at the same time, it deals with issues of entitlements – who decides who is entitled to participate and in which form. Coherence requires that policies and action must be coherent and easily understood. Coherence requires political leadership and a strong responsibility on the part of the institutions to ensure a consistent approach within a complex system (Commission of the European Communities, 2001: 10).

Global governance as an issue became prominent in the 1990s and accelerated after that with the emergence of the financial crisis, which had far-reaching effect on the East Asian economies, but its effect reciprocated also over the rest of the world. There were reasons for the acceleration. First, there were new problems, which can only be solved by collective action at the global level. These new problems got manifested in terms of global terrorism, war and anarchy that affected more than one country, religious fundamentalism and searching for asylum in another country, a space less information system, inability of laws meant to rule a nation to go beyond its geographic boundary, environmental questions and many others. Second, there had been new and enhanced perceptions about the need to manage events internationally. These included sharing river water and other resources like forests and mountains that passed through more than one country, a global common space and nation-state's boundaries, and control over the specified coastal belt, including the oceanic zone.

The antecedents of Global Governance included the debate on the New International Economic Order in the 1970s; the North-South summits of the early 1980s; the United Nations Conference on Environment and Development negotiations in Rio de Janeiro in 1992; and the chain of ensuring UN conferences throughout the decade – the Vienna Conference on Human Rights (14-25 June 1993), the Cairo Conference on Population and Development (5-13 Sept. 1994), the Social Summit at Copenhagen (5-12 March, 1995), and the Beijing Conference on Gender and Development (5-9 June 1995) (web sites). The financial crisis of the 1990s revealed the vulnerability of the emerging market economies. In response to this, the G-7 called for reforms in the global financial architecture by creating the Financial Stability Forum and the global policy institution, G-20, that included economies affected by this financial crisis.

Global governance by institutions should aim at creating arrangements, both formal and informal, to bring about predictability, stability and efficiency in managing the social, economic and political behaviour in any society. This had to develop institutions for implementing the objectives and the policy agenda for which these institutions had been formed. The frame of laws, rules and procedures were developed as instruments of execution of the agenda (Planning Commission, 2002-2007, p. 178). Governance may be state-specific, specific to union of states (like that of the EU), specific to grassroots organizations and corporations, and it may be beyond the state, civil society within the geographic boundary of a politically sovereign country, and the corporations. The type of globalization that we talk about here includes a multiplicity of actors who express their interests through global policy institutions. These actors were not only countries, but also unions of countries like the EU, development-finance institutions like the Breton Woods twins and the trade institution like the WTO. The governance is for decisions on public policy at the global level.

For effective functioning, global governance requires institutions. The apex institution for this purpose since the end of the Second World War was the United Nations (UN). While the UN provided a common platform for all the countries to act by membership, there were policy coordination institutions formed voluntarily by like-minded countries that affected the global course of action. Governance aimed at preventing decisional impasse and implementation failures. Since the countries as members happened to be the catalysts in the decision-making processes, hence they needed to be the participants right from the stage of policy formulation processes in these institutions.

Indicators of Governance

There is no fixed set of indicators of governance. Rather, the set depends on the perspective and the context. Ultimately, however, good governance is democratic governance (UNDP, 2002: 51). This democratic governance is to be read as inclusive governance where all the concerned elements participate consciously and willingly with full information about how the elements are going to be affected by the decisions to be arrived at. The question is not about the competence of an individual/institution/country to participate, but to ensure through increasing participation the development of conscious participation and hence ultimately to develop democracy. Failure of democracy in practice is not to give up democratic values and principles but to reinforce it with more critical reasoning and tolerance for the dissidents. Tolerance and honouring the minority population by language, religion, belief or of a few nations outside the 'conventional democracy' is a function of good governance. Good governance must take care of the people who were subjected to forced cross-border migration and floating citizens under non-normal conditions like ethnic conflicts, religious fundamentalism, etc. This may range from the local-national level to the global level. Good governance should be participatory, consensus-oriented, accountable, transparent, responsive, effective and efficient, equitable and inclusive and in conformity with rules and laws. It should assure that corruption is minimized, the views of minorities are respected and the voices of the most vulnerable in society are respected in decision-making processes. It should also be responsive to the present and future needs of society, that is, its sustainability.

Global Governance is observed to be an attempt to manipulate the forces of globalization, mitigate globalization's negative effects, and privilege states that follow global rules, and globalization, in turn, is a system-level variable (Halabi, 2008: 138). Some of the states, however, were initially privileged by having a lead role in framing global rules for development of a system. Governance aims at stabilizing a system thus built by framing rules and connecting systems. Especially when an international system is in the making or is undergoing transformation, collective decision-making is required by the states set in hierarchy to ensure a transformation visible by transparency. This opposes a closed nature of decision-making process, ensures representation and hence legitimacy (Cooper, 2002: 1-2). The contrasting views get naturally accommodated in this process that accommodates geographical distribution of countries, size of population by each country and the civil society organizations at the national and global level. The collective decision-making promotes the prospect of condominium with an element of collective load-sharing. Thus, governance is linked to building 'order' or setting things in order that is based on legitimacy rather than coercive power. 'In the context of global governance, there is a marked conceptual shift from the concept of state sovereignty to that of popular sovereignty in that the new world order would better reflect the UN charter's aspiration…' (Peou, 2001: 96). Popular sovereignty implies that the government is a representative government (Cohen, 2008, p. 15). In the frame of popular sovereignty, there is 'an ensemble of citizens, of formally and abstractly free and equal individuals set up as political persons, as a source of the state's legitimacy' (Poulantzas, 1968: 277). If the government is representative, it will have reasons to be the ultimate in-charge of internal affairs. The UN Charter of 1945, Article 2(7), upholds the Westphalia principles that there should be no authorization for 'intervention in matters essentially within the domestic jurisdiction of any state' (*The Economist*, 17 May , 2008: 72). Chapter VII of the UN Charter, however, authorizes the Security Council 'to take action in cases of a "threat to the peace, breach of the peace or act of aggression" ' (*The Economist*, 17 May , 2008: 72). This global peace agenda as the supreme guiding determinant of global governance may lead to intervention by global institutions in the state activities. State sovereignty thus remains subject to the scrutiny of the UN Security Council.

At the level of a nation-state, good governance requires impartial enforcement of laws that, in turn, requires an independent judiciary and an impartial and incorruptible public administration. A society's wellbeing depends on ensuring that all its members feel that they have a stake in it and that they do not feel excluded from the mainstream society. Exclusion from the process of governance and political participation is an impoverishment of human lives (Sen, 2004: 31). This requires that all groups, particularly the most vulnerable ones, have opportunities to participate in the processes yielding outcome that affect their lives. Participation may be either direct or through legitimate institutions or representatives. Participation needs to be informed and organized. This means freedom of association and expression on the one hand and an organized civil society on the other. Good Governance means that institutions yield results that meet the needs of society while making the best use of resources at their disposal. It requires that institutions try to serve all stakeholders within a reasonable time frame. Not only the government-run institutions but also the private-run and civil society organizations must be accountable to the public and to their institutional stakeholders. Who is accountable to who varies, depending on whether decisions or actions taken are internal or external to an institution. In general, an institution is accountable to those who will be affected by its decisions or actions. Since the decision-making and its enforcement should follow laws, hence information must be freely available and directly accessible to those who will be affected by enforcement of such decisions. This, in turn, means that the information provided is simple, comprehensible and transparent. The whole process that aims at good governance as a means to long-term end has to be consensus-based in the best interest of the whole community.

Many of the states are in different stages of developing internal democracy. Had governance been only about the rule by law and collective action based on prior informed consent, it would hardly have differed from the efficient functioning of a sovereign state. The international role and response of the sovereign state to international issues are less than the total requirement of Global Governance. Global Governance is basically transnational democracy practiced through institutions that satisfy the criteria of being truly democratic.

As opposed to the 'Washington Consensus' floated in 1989 in the context of Latin American countries based on retreat of the state because of being inefficient (Williamson, 2008: 170-171), post-Washington Consensus put forward a governance agenda that was based on the idea that 'states have important functions in a market-based economy, especially when the concerns for governance centre on social equity and justice questions' (Higgot, 2001: 143). Once the agenda came out from efficiency question and centered on democracy for equity and justice, the governance approach became bottom up as opposed to top down. This may be interpreted also as reinstating Keynesianism to discipline the highest stage of capitalism. The less powerful states as 'rule takers' also got in the process chances to be sharers with 'rule makers'.

The internal nation-specific institutional arrangements also change in response to the globalization project. The nation states today are being 'geared increasingly towards serving the demands and requirements of a process of globalization which is driven not primarily by their political authority but by the multinational corporations and powerful anonymous private traders in the international capital market. …the economic activities of the nation state are being oriented, and many of its economic institutions are being strengthened systematically in the interest of globalization' (Bhaduri, 2002: 42).

The separation of the national constellation from societal denationalization or globalization is doubtful. The issues rooted in international interdependence do not question the formal political sovereignty of the state or the autonomy of the state but surely brings into question the effectiveness of state power. In a denationalizing world with cross-border transactions becoming strengthened more relative to within-border transactions and with the emergence of new social spaces and actors, the convergence of the dimensions of political systems in one political organization vanishes and new governance architecture emerges (Zurn, 2001: 49, 55).

The aspirations of people and the actions of the civil society towards fulfilling those aspirations take the political shape of democracy. 'The democratic revolution of the 1990s that brought representative democracy to almost all of Europe and the Americas continues, with the 1999 conversion of Indonesia into a democratic polity, the 2000 electorally bred change of government in Russia and Mexico…' (Kirton & Takase, 2002:2). As democracy becomes deeper and durable, it becomes the breeding ground for a strengthened civil society that asks for a voice in decision-making. It asks for more transparency, inclusion and accountability of the national government. 'It is a demand expressed nationally in many cases where national reconciliation, following at times violent changes of regime, is the immediate imperative. It is manifested internationally in the cadence of protests from 1999 onward at major international economic meetings of ministers and leaders, where the common demand is for more open decision making so that a broader array of communities and values can have a greater voice' (Kirton &Takase, 2002: 2). Civil society at local and global levels, thus, may have a role in taming not only the rising power of the state but also the power of the cluster of states.

Collective management by consensus or governance at dual levels, national and global, were often mixed when the 'external factors increasingly interact with domestic economic policy' (Bayne, 2002: 21). For example, the TNCs originating from the DMEs might see the developing world as a space for scramble or vying for competitive dominance. The operations of international non-government organizations (INGOs), TNCs and international civil society organizations in a national economy required governance at both the national and global levels in a symbiotic relationship.

The problem for an unequal world by relative location of nation states is that even the core institutions in the subordinate (and often failing) states may fail to act and protect sovereignty as can the institutions in the lead countries. Historically, the decolonized countries of post-Second World War period could not dare to bypass the global outcome for any step they initiated and hence remained at the mercy of global institutions for correction of steps as the latter decide. The indicators accepted as measures of good governance at the national level of these subordinate countries, thus, could not be seen in separation from the authority of the superpower and the indicators that she decided by influence but accepted as consensus in the global institutions.

Even without surrendering the right to govern in a specified territory the sovereign states might agree to form supranational institutions like the European Commission, the European Parliament and the European Court of Justice that were expected to address issues for good governance of the member countries constituting the European Union. The member countries in this case did not see any conflict between national law-cum-state authority and Union's intervention (Zurn, 2001: 66). Parallel to state sovereignty, the supranational institutions enjoyed 'delegated sovereignty' that does not aim at jeopardizing the former. It is opined that 'Europe ...is founded on the very idea of pooled sovereignty' (The Economist, 7 June , 2008: 57). Pooled sovereignty works 'when governments agree to decide future matters by voting procedures other than unanimity' (Zurn, 2001: 79). Even within the frame of pooled sovereignty, one may dislike to share same regional issues with the other. Global governance had to take care of reciprocal state sovereignty that operated in a relative sense.

Why is Governance needed?

If globalization affects all, it 'must be managed so that its fundamentally benign effects are ensured and reinforced' (Bhagwati, 2004: 35). Governance is managing globalization. 'The rapid integration of the global economy in recent decades springs from the widespread recognition that economies invariably achieve more working with each other – exchanging goods, capital, and ideas – than acting alone' (World Bank, 1996: 140). Working with each other presupposes the separate existence and identity of the national economies represented by the state. In an unequal power relation between countries 'working with each other' does not necessarily imply working on equal terms for equal benefits. In case of derived unequal benefits, the aim of economies 'achieving more' remains questionable if 'achievement' is supposed to be uniform.

Functioning of the national economies in the integrated global economy requires a uniform code of conduct for the participating economies. National laws are adequate if geographic space and economic space continue to coincide. Globalization extends the economic space much beyond the geographic space so much so that national rules cannot tackle problems emanating from increasing openness (Nayyar, 2002b: 12). The formulation of the code of conduct requires consensus-based decisions through global bodies. 'Regimes in themselves cannot provide governance structure because they lack the most critical component of governance – the power to enforce compliance. Regimes must rest instead on a political base established through leadership and cooperation. ...regimes governing economic affairs cannot function without a strong leader or hegemon. ...the leader or hegemon facilitates international cooperation and prevents defection from the rules of the regime...' (Gilpin, 2001: 97). The dominant economic power is supposed to accept this leadership role for coordination of macroeconomic policies among the leading economies.

Hegemonic stability requires, for functioning of liberal international economy, a leader that uses its resources and influence to establish and manage an economic order based on free trade, monetary stability, and freedom of movement of capital. The leader must also encourage other states to obey the rules and regimes governing international economic activities (Gilpin, 2001: 99-100). The argument is that the hegemon is supposed to have power and right to monitor the compliance of rules by the states in the rest of the world. This is contradictory because the hegemon framed the code of conduct, took token consent from the other participants and passed it as consensus.

There are at least two approaches of analysis on governance. One is within the nation-state centered on national laws and institutions. If the political frame of the nation state is based on democracy, the logic of governance is all-encompassing. Beyond the national boundary, global governance is centered on global institutions. So far there is no global Parliament and no uniform rule for compliance by all countries. Also, the membership of countries in global institutions is voluntary, provided that the entry is open, thereby the question of compliance does not hold good. Governance comes in the development agenda within a nation-state because, other factors remaining present, absence of good governance may lead to missed development opportunities. 'The universally accepted features of good governance are the exercise of legitimate political power; and formulation and implementation of policies and programmes that are equitable, transparent, non-discriminatory, socially sensitive, participatory and above all accountable to the people at large' (Planning Commission, 2002-2007: 177).

The increased frequency of financial crises, involving even countries with a record of good governance and macroeconomic discipline, shows that instability is global. Although there is room to improve national institutions, that alone would not be sufficient to deal with the crises, particularly in the Third World developing countries, where the potential threat posed by inherently unstable capital flows is much greater. Both the strengthening of national-level institutions and building up institutions at the international level are essential if the threat of such crises is to be reduced and if they are to be better managed whenever they occur (UNCTAD, 2001: 61).

The institutions at the national and international levels are set up by participation of the people/countries that are meant to govern the nation-state and the integration of nation-states in a single whole. The institutions need to be accountable to their constituents. The global institutions can connect better with governments of national economies, democratically elected representatives and civil society. It is neither feasible nor desirable for any single nation or individual to go alone. The national governments in practice share responsibilities via international treaties and institutions. The danger comes if these institutions lack accountability, ownership, scrutiny and political maturity (Moore, 2003: 217). Thus, institutions for global governance need to be created. This is not to be confused with global government. In fact, governance is for ensuring global democracy.

In 1945 the UN was founded with 51 member countries considered as a political center for global governance for all issues that affect member states. Now the membership in UN has almost quadrupled. For any relevant issue making an assembly of representatives of member states of the UN and allowing each of them to present views for less than five minutes in the General Assembly will not carry much operational meaning. Particularly on issues that need changes by setting up of new institutions including institutional reforms, one may be prone to think outside the UN umbrella. These reforms include ensuring stability in financial markets, correcting the built-in bias in the existing international trade and financial institutions that favour developed countries, and ensuring high quality public life (Moore, 2003: 224, 226).

The major economic decisions that affected the world economy were taken by the governments of the industrialized countries who held the main decision-making power in the institutions that "govern" the global economy (www.sice.oas.org, 7 May, 2004). The functioning of the world economy required the institutions of global economic governance to practice specialization and division of labour. That is, each institution should be responsible for a specific area of activity to prevent overlapping jurisdiction and the resulting lack of accountability. The reason for this was not just that clarity of responsibility is conducive to efficiency, but also because confusion about responsibilities favoured the countries in power that could play one organization against another in a process of divide-and-rule (Griffin, 2003: 798).

All the heads of State and Government that assembled in Monterrey, Mexico, on 21 – 22 March , 2002, resolved unanimously that 'Good governance is essential for sustainable development. Sound economic policies, solid democratic institutions responsive to the needs of the people and improved infrastructure are the basis for sustained economic growth, poverty reduction and employment creation. Freedom, peace and security, domestic stability, respect for human rights, including the right to development, and the rule of law, gender equality, market-oriented policies, and an overall commitment to just and democratic societies are also essential and mutually reinforcing' (United Nations, 2002: 69).

What came out from the different views on governance was that the observers-cum-viewers differed on the concept when governance was domain-specific. If it was intra-nation, the role and functions of the institutions got prominence; while if it was inter-nation, the role of the leader (country) and leading group got prominence. While the institutions were supposed to be accountable to the nation (within the nation), it was not clear whom the leader was accountable to. It is also not very clear how the leader looked into development opportunities, and whose development opportunities were sought for.

World Institutions

'Institutions are rules, enforcement mechanisms, and organizations. ...Distinct from policies, which are the goals and desired outcomes, institutions are the rules, including behavioural norms, by which agents interact – and the organizations that implement rules and codes of conduct to achieve desired outcomes. Policies affect which institutions evolve – but institutions too affect which policies are adopted. Institutional structure affects behaviour. But behaviour may also change within existing institutional structures' (World Bank, WDR, 2002: 6). If governance means equitable distribution of vulnerability of economies and people therein, the institutions are the agents through which rules for the purpose get executed. In other words, governance and institutions are inseparable.

An economy is always in the making. In this sense, there is no rigid frame or boundary an economy has taken forever. Just as the economic agents give shape to institutions, so also institutions play catalytic roles in this making of the economy. The functioning of the institutions leads to complex spatiality of governance and regulation. These encompass the diverse spaces and spatial scales (national, supranational and sub-national) of state organizations and institutions within civil society. Nation-states play a critical role in governance and regulation (Hudson, 2004: 453).

A structured and functioning institutional system at the global level requires that 'reforms in global and regional institutions are complemented by reforms in national institutions and policies. In that sense, there must be a basic consistency between the global economic regime promoted by the global institutions and the policy regimes at national level. ...global priorities and global rules of the game, must ultimately be consistent with the national priorities of developed, developing and transition economies' (www.sice.oas.org, May 7, 2004). The global institutions execute the rules that cover stabilizing the global structure, reducing uncertainty, promoting efficiency, and, hence, ensuring stronger performance. The operational domains are economy, society and polity. The regional space ranges from local to global. The most powerful agencies promoting policy liberalization had been the two Breton Woods institutions, through their stabilization and structural adjustment programmes, specific developmental goals and general policy advice (Lall, 2002: 95). In the context of the need of institutions at the level of the national economy, the IMF suggested three measures why and how institutions could play a positive role towards the ends. The first was the quality of governance. The second was the extent of legal protection of private property and how well such laws were enforced. The third was the level of institutional and other limits on political leaders (IMF, April 2003, WEO: 97). The question, however, remained about designing national policy packages that ensure national autonomy, for example, in pursuing policy objectives of full employment, stable growth and a more equitable income distribution. The voice of the marginalized people within the marginalized countries might remain unheard in the global policy institutions. For the member countries in the global policy institutions, uniformity in policy means, for example, if free trade is in the accepted agenda, then the trade regime in all the member countries has to be based on free trade. This does not, however, imply that the non-members remain privileged by protecting the choice of national autonomous policy path. The task that remained for the countries not included so far in the major policy institutions was to seek a berth, and as early as possible, in the policy institutions.

When we talk about the role of the member countries in global governance through global policy institutions in particular, the history and hence the evolution of the rules of the game should be considered. This is because while some of the member countries could understand the implications of the rules as executed, some other countries remained at the back. This is, in turn, because of the colonizer's differential treatment of the colonies. The seventeenth century to nineteenth century European colonization of the then developing world showed two types of colonies. One was the "settler colonies" where well-populated settlements of Europeans accompanied by institutions to ensure property rights, enforced the rule of law, and hence supported investment and growth (examples include the United States, Australia, and New Zealand). The other was the "extractive colonies" where there was much more limited migration and establishment instead of local elite, and the institutional emphasis was on solidifying colonial control and supporting the extraction of natural resources. This included most of sub-Saharan Africa and Latin America. As viewed by the IMF, colonial origins had long-term effects on the form and strength of institutions in the countries concerned, and hence on economic performance in general. 'Institutions in much of central and South America were designed to concentrate power in the hands of an elite whereas in North America, institutions allowed for and encouraged much broader participation in economic and political activity' (IMF, April, 2003, WEO: 100). Thus, institutions had different roles in different countries. In one type the institutions worked in a frame of concentrated elite-centered power while in the other it opened up broader democratic participation. It also reveals the formation and functioning of an institutional system. 'The civil law framework inherited from continental Europe, particularly France, has tended to produce a larger role for the state, higher regulatory burden, and less flexible and adaptable legal and economic institutions – holding back financial development, for example. In contrast, common law practices stemming from British colonization have been associated with more adaptable institutions and greater protection of investors –both from state appropriation and from corporate insiders' (IMF, April, 2003, WEO: 100). Thus, what we conceive of as institution's functions are reflections of how they were derived, and from what source. Generally, we have in mind Europe, with two leaders, Britain and France, when we talk about rigidity and flexibility in the institutional system.

The point of concern is that when the decolonized countries participate as members in global policy institutions, the historically derived non-uniformity or uneven economic location of the national economies may obstruct them from working in cohesion in a single body. Conflicts and differences may also come between global rules and local/national rules. Poor governance was a major weakness in Asia's (minus Japan) financial and corporate sectors. The symptoms included intricate formal and informal relationships between governments, financial institutions, and corporations; inadequate disclosure requirements; and widespread corruption (ADB, 2000: 35). Under the guidance of the institutions like the Asian Development Bank, the IMF, and the World Bank, the countries in crisis started focusing on governance at the national-local levels. These included reform actions on increasing the transparency of economic and financial matter, strengthening corporate disclosure requirements, increasing accountability to shareholders, strengthening competition laws, privatizing state-owned enterprises, dismantling monopolies and cartels, and restructuring opaque corporate relations (ADB, 2000: 35).

The institutions which were at the center of governance were judged by the norms they adopted and executed. At an international level they were the development-finance-trade related institutions (World Bank-IMF-WTO) as well as the institution for justice, peace and equity (UN), just as at the national level they were the institutions under and associated with state control. At the national level they were the executing arms of the state and the judiciary. For credibility and legitimacy to the members, citizens and people at large, these institutions at both the levels should perform in such a way as to make the stake holders convinced that the decisions for execution are consensus-based.

About the Book

This book is a collection of four lectures encompassing both economic and non-economic viewpoints by well known scholars. There is no comparison on the relative strength of these viewpoints. Each author decided

His own domain and delivered lectures that have given the scope to compile and present it in a book form. **Jan Breman** opines that 'the meaning of exclusion is to be denied value, to have no constructive role to play in economic or non-economic terms, to be in excess to demand. Social systems based on the norms of equality, on the other hand, do not easily tolerate exclusion. If, for some unforeseen reasons, people have stopped being included, the prevalent reaction is to facilitate their return to the included fold. In the world at large, and this also has to do with the process of globalization, there seems to be a trend from exclusion towards inclusion, if not in practice, then at least as a social ideal, that need universal promotion. Exclusion in the sense of being denied the right to have access to inclusion may have last whatever legitimacy it earlier had'. He suggested looking at 'the exclusion-inclusion divide not as a fixed polarity but as a continuum, a sliding scale which is subject to changes over time. What needs to be added here is that also the awareness of exclusion, or for that matter inclusion, is not static but dynamic. Questions to be raised are not only exclusion from what and by whom but also since when. Finally, as important is the perception of exclusion by the excluded in the perception of exclusion by the included. What are the overt and covert scripts for keeping the excluded part of mankind hidden from becoming visible and exercising their human rights and to end the violation of their human rights?'

Breman refutes the long-held theory that the social sector is a characteristic feature of urban economic activity, to the extent that there is social duality, the tendency to split into two sectors manifests itself in a way that transcends the dynamics of the urban economy. By drawing the same distinction in the rural economy it is possible to identify the ties between formal and informal segments in town and hinterland - manifested in the circulation of both labour and capital - and include them in an analysis of the economic order as a whole. He rejects the view that informality refers largely or exclusively to self-employment. What often appears to be own-account work is in fact some form of wage labour, for orders contracted out by intermediaries such as sub-contractors or jobbers. Both in small-scale enterprises and in the chain of dependency made up of brokers and ending with home workers, wages are paid not on an hourly basis, but by piecework. To record this as self-employment is to overlook the fact that such labouring modalities actually bear the hallmark of an employer-employee relationship expressed in the form of wage payment.

In view of **Kamal Nayan Kabra**, 'Globalization penetrates the inner essence, motivation and actual operation of national and international politics. With its strong centralization in the economic, political, military and informational fields, paradoxically, it is supposed to be consistent with the somewhat divergent trends towards more effective federalization and decentralization of politics, giving credence to the quip: think global, act local in the interest of good governance'.

Kabra opines, 'A common thread seen across all the diverse concepts of globalization is the large-scale, growing and unhindered free flow of resources, goods and services, ideals, natural and legal persons, financial claims in the form of various old and new instruments characteristic of the present day corpulent and predominant, financial sector across national boundaries, whether in fact or as preferred courses at the level of policy permitted options. Thus, it appears that the essence of globalization is a borderless world - virtual global village. In this concept, clearly the unit of analysis is, of course, the nation- state. But at the ground level the preponderate proportion of activities which constitute international economic relations do not have nations as the operative, directly decision-making units. All these formerly controlled and regulated and now under globalization free cross-border activities are the activities of either natural or legal persons, who are the primary entities making decisions and, consequently, gaining or losing from them? True, the nation state provides the legal and policy framework for these activities the same way as it does for the domestic activities, except for the complications arising from separate national origins of the entities involved. Thus the nation state enters the picture for determining the external sector policies and procedures, while the operational, micro decision-making entities are the natural and legal persons. Apparently, this mismatch has not emerged accidentally and has identifiable implications'.

Kabra continues, 'The state activities which find favour with the globalists are those which facilitate and encourage cross border, unrestricted movements of goods, services and financial resources according to the preset economic needs of the rich, industrialized countries, mainly the G-7 countries and the big MNEs originating and controlled from them". In view of Kabra, 'Even in the economic sphere, instead of the real economy, it is the financial sector with its astronomical size of daily cross border transactions (apparently the leading sector of the presently reigning globalization) which is the heart of the present-day globalization. These speculative, casino-like financial supermarkets are the playgrounds of the rich mainly from the rich OECD countries, but with a very volatile and mercurial presence in some select poor but large economies. Everywhere these financial markets are dominated by the electronic herd like "faceless stock, bond and currency traders sitting behind computer screens all over the globe moving their money around from mutual funds to pension funds to emerging market fund, or trading on the Internet from their basements". It is mammon-worship by these speculators who could not care less about the real economy implications of their games'.

In the view of **Rajmohan Gandhi**, 'Economic growth under the modern civilization has created immense pressure on the natural resource base such as land, forest, water and air. Overexploitation and pollution are two menaces in the context of the use of both renewable and non-renewable natural resources. A new movement, namely, environment movement has emerged, and it is fairly powerful. Morality and values have been brought to discussion via the irreversible damages being caused to the nature. The conventional development models have supposedly led to disaster and destruction' To him, 'Globalization means onslaught of foreign capital and technology destroying the inland systems of production, exploitation of workers in the poor countries and most importantly, cultural invasion and market expansion. ..... it is really happening and will ultimately undermine the autonomy and authority of nation states. Multinational National Companies (MNCs) are specially targeted for attack and its postulation that the MNCs will ultimately undermine the authority of the nation state. The debate in literature on the cultural invasion and market expansion has brought out that the main player that is also definitely gaining is America. In fact, the perceived threat is 'Americanization'. Rajmohan Gandhi quotes extensively from the writings of Mahatma Gandhi to critically examine globalization as economic globalization.

The article penned by **Ramashray Roy** deals with life and good life. In his view, 'If the term "life" refers to a life devoted to the satisfaction of ordinary life needs, the term "good life" underlines the need for every man to grow to the full stature of humanity the seeds of which are implanted deep in the being. This does not by any means signify the negation of the basic concerns of the pragmatic dimensions of existence. It only means to be alive to the demands of the intellectual and spiritual aspects of life. Man's being in its totality is represented by a complex of body, mind, and spirit; it is necessary for every individual to cater to the needs of his total being. If, for any reason, one of these elements receives greater or fuller attention as compared to others, the holistic pattern of the development of man to the fullest extent of his potentialities gets distorted. This distortion affects not only his internal psychic balance but also the pattern of his relationship with the external world, both society and nature'. The rest of the article elaborated on the above.

Content

Globalization, Poverty and Exclusion

Jan Breman

The Notion of Exclusion

My point of departure is the concept of exclusion defined as the lack of access to full participation in mainstream society in economic, political, social and cultural terms. Exclusion conveys a sense of denial or loss of access to a life of dignity. The focus in this paper is on the relationship between globalization and exclusion: to what extent is globalization instrumental in overcoming or aggravating situations of exclusion? To reach meaningful answers to this question, it is necessary to understand both phenomena in a historical perspective. Exclusion is certainly not of recent origin and cannot only be related to the acceleration in the process of globalization during the last quarter of a century. At the same time, the hierarchy of inequality of the transnational level can only be understood by analyzing the historical trajectory of globalization.

The condition of exclusion under which people work and live is often operationalized in terms of poverty and inequality. The first dimension refers to lack of assets. Given the absence of a substantial segment of the workforce of means of production such as land or other forms of capital to gain income, people must sell their labour power for their living. Poverty becomes particularly acute if firstly, the price of labour, calculated in monetary or non-monetary terms, is close to or even below the level of reproduction and second, if unemployment or underemployment is rampant because the supply of labour is structurally much higher than the demand. If often happens that these two factors are interdependent. Exclusion from means of production can lead to exclusion from means of consumption. In those cases the state of marginality and vulnerability takes the shape of a pauperized existence. I shall elaborate on these issues on the basis of the anthropological fieldwork which I have conducted during the past four decades in a variety of urban and rural locations in South and Southeast Asia.

There are various dimensions to exclusion which do not necessarily overlap. In an economic sense exclusion refers to the inability to be engaged in gainful employment which yields enough income for satisfying basic requirements. In political terms exclusion implies lack of access to sources of power, the inability to participate meaningfully in decision-making processes from the household level upwards. In a social sense, if exclusion is equal to denigration, the loss of respectability and dignity in the eyes of self as well as of others. Discrepancy between these three dimensions provides room for interventions which became universalized after decolonization in South and Southeast Asian societies increased the political leverage of social classes which until then had remained without voice. To that extent the introduction of democracy increased the room for maneuver for social segments - for instance agricultural labourers in India - which remained stuck at the bottom of rural economy and society. Experience has shown, however, that a democratic framework is not a sufficient condition for inclusion. Neither does the absence of democracy necessarily imply that no action is taken to remove conditions of stark poverty.

When the various dimensions of exclusion reinforce each other, a pattern of accumulated exclusion arise which is difficult to tackle. Just like the category of the super or ultra-poor which has been recently distinguished in literature, it might make sense to identify an underclass of the super- or ultra-excluded. Characteristic for such situations is that the various dimensions of vulnerability conflate in segregation, i.e. a kind of separation from mainstream society which also has a spatial connotation.

Poverty is not a sufficient condition for exclusion. People may suffer from deprivation but if they are not able to relate their own circumstances to conditions in which other people live there is no reason for them to feel excluded. Globalization as a process has certainly helped to extend social horizons and to increase aspirations. The new means of communication that have emerged makes it easier for people to relate the (inferior) quality of their own life to the superior standards which other people, nearby or far away, enjoy. Relative deprivation is, thus, of enormous significance in the definition of exclusion. Of course, social systems for which hierarchy is the organizing principle are characterized by a skewed distribution of property, power and prestige. But can people positioned at the bottom of such societies automatically be characterized as the excluded? In the earlier literature on caste order in South Asia the conventional opinion was to define such categories in terms of exclusion: the out-castes, those living beyond the pale, etc. In socio-economic terms, however, these categories were very much included since their presence as well as the economic services they performed were required for the higher castes to retain their purity. The meaning of exclusion is to be denied value, to have no constructive role to play in economic or non-economic terms, to be in excess to demand. Social systems based on the norms of equality, on the other hand, do not easily tolerate exclusion. If, for some unforeseen reasons, people have stopped being included, the prevalent reaction is to facilitate their return to the included fold. In the world at large, and this also has to do with the process of globalization, there seems to be a trend from exclusion towards inclusion, if not in practice, then at least as a social ideal, that need universal promotion. Exclusion in the sense of being denied the right to have access to inclusion may have last whatever legitimacy it earlier had.

To juxtapose exclusion in opposition to inclusion is detrimental to our understanding of both. As in all variations on the concept of dualism, focusing on the contrasts helps us to understand that in real life the essence lies on what is in between. My suggestion is to look at the exclusion-inclusion divide not as a fixed polarity but as a continuum, a sliding scale which is subject to changes over time. What needs to be added here is that also the awareness of exclusion, or for that matter inclusion, is not static but dynamic. Questions to be raised are not only exclusion from what and by whom but also since when. Finally, as important is the perception of exclusion by the excluded in the perception of exclusion by the included. What are the overt and covert scripts for keeping the excluded part of mankind hidden from becoming visible and exercising their human rights and to end the violation of their human rights?

Globalization and the Promise of Inclusion

Wallerstein's seminal work on the emergence of the world system addresses many biases in the interpretation of globalization as a recent phenomenon. For all criticisms raised by him, however, this sociologist seems to agree that the development path followed in the third world is essentially a repetition of the transformation process that took place in the Atlantic societies during the 19th and the first half of the 20th century. His analysis suggests a transition in the last few decades from agrarian-rural economies to industrial-urban economies. His skepticism mainly concerns the sustainability of the capitalist mode of production at the global 'De-realization' is how Wallerstein has summed up this process, which has drastically changed the composition of the global economy in the last half century. According to him, a vast labour army, until the recent past firmly engaged in agricultural production and living in the countryside, has managed to reach the cities where they become absorbed in the informal economy before moving on to the formal sector. The optimistic statement made by Wallerstein is that having become accustomed to this non-agrarian work, regardless of the variable need for it which results in bouts of unemployment, in the end leads to a higher wage level. For the labourers engaged in this mode of existence, the experience they, thus, gain is the take-off for their next transfer to the formal sector of the economy. 'Even where there are large numbers of persons who are technically unemployed and deriving their income, such as it is, from the informal economy, the real alternatives available to workers located in the barrios and favelas of the world system are such that they are in a position to demand reasonable wage levels to enter the formal wage economy.' (Wallerstein, 2000: 262)

Wallerstein's analysis characterizes the informal sector in the urban economy as a waiting room, a transitional entry point from where, after a certain time, rural migrants succeed in climbing up to more dignified work in the city by upgrading their skills and strengthening their bargaining position. In the accounts of my recurrent research in West Java (Indonesia) and in South Gujarat (India), I have pointed out that large contingents of the land-poor and landless underclass pushed out from agriculture and a rural existence are forced to remain on the march between town and countryside as well as between different economic sectors and various employment modalities. Footloose labour is the term I have used to highlight the nomadic work and life patterns of this reserve army, which has left home but is unable to find a new habitat immediately or even after many years and has most certainly failed to pave its way to the formal sector of the urban economy. The shift that has come about should not be understood, in my opinion, as basically indicating a repetition of the same process of urban-industrial restructuring which in an earlier epoch came about in the North Atlantic basin. The exodus from the village economy in the third world, a concept which has rapidly lost its analytical and policy relevance, does not mean that the swelling numbers of migrants succeed in settling down in urban locations. Although in sheer size of population the big cities have grown more rapidly than ever before, large contingents remain involved in a process of labour circulation. Such patterns of mobility are irrespective of distance, sometimes linking place of origin and destination within one country or stretching in other instances across continental boundaries. The incessant flow and perpetual rotation are related to employment regimes marked by either self-account work or waged labour, in the latter case more often based on casual rather than regular contracts. The need for highly flexibilized labour market behaviour coincides with payment for task which requires little or no skills and schooling. Such are, in sum, the conditions characteristic for a wide range of activities in the informal sector of the economy (Breman, 1996, 2002).

I now return to the analysis of Wallerstein based on the assumption that world capitalism is in an acute and even terminal state of crisis. The ongoing expansion of this mode of production is, according to this sociologist, frustrated by an economic reversal caused by a substantial fall in the profit margins. The resulting pressure implies a squeeze on the accumulation of capital which always has been the organizing principle of capitalism. The investments needed for broadening and deepening markets are drying up. The first of the three factors responsible for the economic turn-around has already been mentioned: rising wages all over the world which make it impossible for capital to 'run away' to regions still 'underdeveloped' where the cost of labour is much lower. Capitalist entrepreneurs can no longer adhere to their tested strategy of continuous relocation of production but must confront directly the demands from informal sector workers for more reasonable incomes. The catchment zones of reserve labour in the globalized hinterland, which until now seemed so inexhaustible, have at last been incorporated in the market economy and, after passing through a phase of being socially uprooted and politically in disarray, finally managed to strengthen its bargaining position vis-a-vis capital and exert upward a fairly optimistic assessment which I find difficult to tally with the sustained poverty of the lower strata in rural and urban India. To an even lesser degree I have seen these people entering the formal waged economy, as is suggested by Wallerstein (2000: 261-2).

Do profit levels of capital show a declining trend because of the two other factors discussed by him? Those refer, on the one hand, to the rising inability of private companies not to include waste removal and cleaning up the environment in their price of operation and, on the other hand, the increase in taxation needed for public expenditure. To start with the first source of pressure, the emergence of the ecology movement would imply that firms nowadays must bear themselves the cost of purification of land, water and air. In the areas of my research in South and Southeast Asia such a decisive swing to private accountability would be extremely difficult to discern. The strategy of free enterprise to externalize these costs of pollution seems to go on unabated as far yet. The reluctance of the average state regime in the third world to take strong action against environmental degradation signals, in my opinion, the raw and untamed nature of capitalism in the global periphery. In those large parts of the world, consumer organizations and other non-governmental agencies have been able to build up much less space for exercising public pressure than in the prosperous core zones of capitalism on which Wallerstein seems to rest his case.

A third source of pressure lies in the steady intensification of taxation. Capital is subject to the demand for public security and is, moreover, not any longer in a position to go on blatantly denying popular claims for better education, health care and lifetime insurance. In Wallerstein's judgment, the urge to make these concessions stems from the need to legitimize state action for thus for underprivileged segments of the population and the concomitant realization among the more well to do that such gestures are unavoidable for the sake of further political stability (Wallerstein 2000: 263). Again, in the course of my empirical research in India and Indonesia for the last four decades, I have not come across the fear either among politicians or the bourgeoisie that the lower social strata pose a serious threat to low and order living up to their reputation, gained in an altogether different setting, as *'les classes dangereuses'*. The denigration of the labouring poor, which is the dominant attitude in mainstream society, is not tempered by the idea that there is a hidden repository of countervailing power down below waiting to become mobilized against intolerable exploitation and exclusion.

There is neither a sign of growing support for a more rigorous system of public taxation nor of a shift in the balance of power leading to a more equitable distribution of wealth. The fiscal crisis of states hinted at by Wallerstein (2000:264) has certainly nothing to do with an intolerable burden of taxation to which the non-poor are subjected. For the masses on the vast subcontinent of South Asia the opposite case could be argued: states which are both unable and unwilling to appropriate a reasonable portion of the value added to capital in the process of production or even to exercise adequate control over the ways in which capital is spent. Consequently, no social safety nets are introduced which would help to minimize the vulnerability of poor people while also expenditure on public housing, education and healthcare are much lower than what is minimally required for substantially improving the life standards of informal sector workers.

My conclusion is that the squeeze of capital in the global economy, operationalized by Wallerstein in sharply falling profit rates, does not take place in the setting of my local-level fieldwork during the last forty years in India or Indonesia. Nor have I found evidence of stagnation in the accumulation of capital. According to me, it would be easier to plead in favour of the contrasting thesis, i.e. on acceleration governance. Capital has become significantly more volatile between countries and continents but the ways in which it is maneuvered around has not been accompanied by growing control or even transparency.

Freeing capital of official regulation is paralleled by a concentration of the surplus resulting in a progressive tilting of the balance between the haves and the haves-not. I would reject the suggestion that my findings have no other validity than for the sites of my anthropolitical investigations in a variety of rural and urban locations in both India and Indonesia. As a matter of fact, Wallerstein is very much aware that the trend towards polarization has not really halted. 'The record of post-"revolutionary" regimes has been that they not been able to reduce worldwide or even internal polarization to any significant degree, nor have they been able to institute serious internal political equality. They have, no doubt, accomplished many reforms, but they promised for more than reforms. And because the world system has remained a capitalist world economy, the regimes outside the core zone have been structurally unable to 'catch up' with the wealthy countries'. (2000: 265)

In view of this unequivocal statement, his prediction of a terminal crisis is even more surprising. Without rejecting the term as such, I would like to give it a meaning different from the one he has put forward. In my perception, the true crisis of world capitalism seems to be the stubborn and pernicious unwillingness to enable a very substantial part of making to qualify themselves both as producers and consumers for full and fair participation in the regimen of capitalist activity. The formalization of labour - in the sense of higher wages, job projection and social insurance, all essential ingredients for a more dignified lifestyle - remains absent. The inevitable result is that the much-needed improvement in the bargaining power for the labouring poor does not materialize, which is a precondition for a structural rather than conjectural market expansion.

Mine is an uncomfortable observation which, moreover, does not square easily with the notion that capitalism, more than any other made of production, is based on the logic of rationality. Are prosperity and democracy for a minority of the world population in the long term compatible with the exclusion from these 'goods' of a larger part of mankind condemned to live in dire poverty and subordination deprived from basic needs and elementary human rights? In an elaborate and comprehensive sociological analysis de Swaan has elaborated on the reasons why, and the lines along which the national elites in the North-Atlantic basin towards the end of the nineteenth century decided to admit the labouring poor as full-fledged citizens to mainstream society. At the end of his study the warning comes that the processes of collectivization and civilization which shaped this societal transformation for various reasons but to a large extent also because of the reduced role played by government may not be repeated on the basis of a similar proceeding on a global scale (de Swaan, 1988: 257).

Quite rightly Wallerstein has pointed out the people everywhere in the world is taking back from the states the role of providing for their pawn security (Wallerstein, 2000:265). My comment is that this trend not to surrender the right to exercise violence might have more to do with aggressive than defensive purposes. In other words, such inclination could find its inspiration not in the fear of unruly behaviour of the poor but rather demonstrates elite determination to resort eventually to untamed brutality to consolidate individual or collective gains made and even to widen the gap further by not giving to but taking from the poor. After all, a major trend in the process of globalization is not the alleviation of misery at the bottom end but the progressive enrichment at the top end.

I strongly disagree with Wallerstein's assessment of a terminal crisis of the world capitalist system. One can indeed conclude that a crisis is going on, but the one I discern has to do with the hesitancy of capitalism to deepen markets by increasing the purchasing power of the segments of mankind living in poverty and to put an end to their state of exclusion in terms of both production and consumption.

Informalization

The state of deprivation from basic needs as well as rights easily conjures up an image of helplessness, of people who are failing in the universal human urge to live in dignity and are a burden both to themselves and to others. This need not necessarily suggest that the blame for their sub-human existence lies with the poor themselves, in the sense that they are primarily responsible for their dismal fate. The misery in which at least one fifth of humanity lives - a figure that rises as high as a third or a half in some regions - is after all associated with lack of access to the basic resources that could free them from poverty. Aid from the non-poor can help the poor in their efforts to achieve progress and can even be of critical importance. The idea of development aid - transfer of capital, mainly, from the rich North to the poor South - seemed to bear witness to this sense of generosity in the second half of the twentieth century. The economic policy-makers of the new world order that now exists have also committed themselves to reducing poverty as part of their strategy aimed at perpetual growth. However, it looks like the World Bank, the International Monetary Fund and the World Trade Organization would succeed in their pro-poor mission only if the remedy suggested by these multilateral agencies wins the approval and support of all concerned, beginning with the target group itself. Enlightened self-interest activated through market forces is the undisputed cornerstone of the neo-liberal policy scenario.

Do the habitués of the poor really conform to that golden rule of the globalized economy? The long-cherished argument that poverty is mainly a question of insufficient or inadequate economic activity - whether voluntary or imposed - has become less convincing since the 1970s, when case studies on what is known as the informal sectored in various parts of the world began to reveal the highly active existence of men, women and children crowding at the bottom of the urban economy in Third World countries. This insight has given rise to a new platitude suggesting that unemployment is a luxury poor people cannot afford. I belief the term 'labouring poor' is entirely appropriate for the unregulated and complex community that populates the informal sector landscape.

Although the income of informal sector workers indeed tends to be somewhat higher than the wages earned by agricultural labourers, a clear majority of the former households have still to survive on per capita incomes of less than one US dollar per day. This means that the people dependent on informalized employment are in most cases firmly stuck below the poverty line. According to a somewhat more lenient definition of deprivation, i.e., allowing not only for bare subsistence but also for cost of e.g., for housing, Medicare, education and a modicum of leisure, this level is fixed at a per capital amount of expenditure of at least two dollars per capita per day, not incidentally but regularly. Such existence in 'comfort' is quite exceptional outside the realm of the formal sector.

The 'discovery' of the informal sector in the urban economy at the beginning of the 1970s went together with the assumption that this zone functioned as a waiting room in which the army of migrants originating from the hinterland could adjust themselves to their new milieu before making their way up to the formal sector where they find higher qualified better paid, more secure and protected jobs. Based on my recurrent empirical investigations, I conclude that cases of such upwardly mobile trajectories are difficult to find. A series of policy reports in the 1970s and 1980s, commissioned mainly by the International Labour Organization (ILO), drew attention to what was called the informal sector problem, suggesting measures and regulations to upgrade work and life conditions of the working poor in third world countries. The same type of analyses and the remedial schemes that accompany them are still being written.

This benign strategy, however, has been gradually replaced by the opinion that labour markets in poor countries need more, and not less, flexibilization. From that direction comes the suggestion to abolish what is called the unfair and unjust privileging of labour in the formal sector of the economy. The protection of a small but powerful vanguard of the workforce should stop and, for the sake of stimulating growth of employment, governments are exhorted to facilitate the free interplay of market forces. In the same line of thinking, there is no room for introducing state-initiated schemes of social provisions. These recommendations were made by the World Bank in a major policy document. I have critically reviewed the substance of the World Development Report 1995 and the argumentation along the same line maintaining that the informal sector is the solution rather than the problem argues that what looks like poverty, defined as lack of property, on closer inspection is a misrepresentation of capital formation that does take place, as a matter of fact on an impressive scale in the informal sector of the economy. I strongly disagree with this partly exaggerated and partly misleading appraisal (Breman, 2002).

Since the introduction of the informal sector concept, opinion has been divided as to its social impact. Some authors, inclined to a more positive assessment, have pointed to the accelerated shift in livelihood patterns away from agriculture and villages to cities and towns that has occurred in large parts of the Third World since the mid-twentieth century. Even if the masses of migrants flooding into urban areas were lucky enough to find their feet, the vast majority of them could gain no access to the formal sector. It was still too small to cope immediately with the continuous influx of newcomers. Under the circumstances the informal sector acted as a catchment reservoir for the jobseekers who has been forced out of their rural agricultural existence. In this interpretation, the emphasis is on the stamina, the flexibility, the will to adapt, the ingenuity and the attempts made for upward mobility of the footloose workforce flooding into Third World cities. The more integrated they became in their new milieu of work and life and the more skills they acquired, the better qualified they would be for the formal sector of the economy, and in making this leap forward they would form trade unions to strengthen their bargaining power with both employers and the government.

The more critical analysis of researchers who have observed that the formal sector remained inaccessible for reasons other than the inferior quality of the new urbanites labour, and their other defects, contrasts with this optimistic view. The failure of the newcomers efforts to find stable and reasonably paid work was due mainly to a development strategy that, in the face of excess supply, sought to keep the price of labour as low as possible, allowed no room for collective action to reduce these people's vulnerability and refused to provide this footloose workforce with government assistance. In short, the lack of registration, organization and protection does not have its origin in the free play of social forces but is the product of economic interests that benefit from the state of informality in which a wide range of activities in all branches of the economy are kept, systematically and on a large scale, through evasion of labour laws and taxation.

I share this last interpretation and my empirical research findings contradict the dominant image of the informal sector as a separate and closed circuit of work and labour. To fully understand the mechanism that underlies economic transfers, we must focus on the interaction between the formal and informal sectors, and particularly on the dependence of the latter on the former, and its subordination to it. To start with, I refute the long-held theory that there is social sector is a characteristic feature of urban economic activity. To the extent that there is social duality, the tendency to split into two sectors manifests itself in a way that transcends the dynamics of the urban economy. By drawing the same distinction in the rural economy, it is possible to identify the ties between formal and informal segments in town and hinterland - manifested in the circulation of both labour and capital - and include them in an analysis of the economic order as a whole. I also reject the view that informality refers largely or exclusively to self-employment. What often appears to be own-account work is in fact some form of wage labour, for orders contracted out by intermediaries such as (sub) contractors or jobbers. Both in small-scale enterprises and in the chain of dependency made up of brokers and ending with home workers, wages are paid not on an hourly basis, but by piecework. To record this as self-employment is to overlook the fact that such labouring modalities bear the hallmark of an employer-employee relationship expressed in the form of wage payment.

The different views on the informal sector did not stop most studies focusing, until recently, on its time-bound nature. Whatever the school of thought the authors adhered to, they almost always felt they could assume that informality was a temporary phenomenon born of the slow expansion of the formal sector economy. The acceleration that would inevitably happen would lead to a simultaneous shrinking of the informal sector. This prognosis came from the assumption of parallel development whereby the process of transformation seen in the Third World in the second half of the twentieth century would essentially follow the same route already travelled by developed societies. The formalization of industrial activity was bound to lead to technological modernization and organizational expansion, while the productivity of services would also increase as capital was added. This transformation should be accompanied by growing state involvement designed to increase public control over the use of capital, labour and other resources. The silenced informal sector workers would gain a voice in society by taking collective action to represent their own interests. These analyses, made in the 1970s, seem to have last more of their currency over the years.

The fact that the informal sector has continued to grow rather than declining in magnitude and significance is undoubtedly the most obvious indication of this reverse trend. The earlier estimates that less than half the working population lived on the proceeds of the informal sector have since been revised to include more than three-quarters of all those who are gainfully employed. A complex of economic and social mechanisms has led to a rapid fall in the volume of labour in agriculture. Displacement to other areas of economic activity in both urban and rural areas has occurred under conditions characteristic of work in the informal sector, which I have summarized as sustained mobility, no stable but casual work and piecework rather than time-rate employment (Breman, 1996). The growing pressure in the bottom layers of the economy outside agriculture has not been relieved by the expansion of formal sector employment. There are in fact signs that this segment has shrunk over the past few decades.

The recognition of this unexpected dynamic has led to a reconsideration of the view that the process of economic growth in the Third World is essentially a delayed repetition of the industrialization and urbanization scenario that laid the foundations for the Western welfare state in the early twentieth century. This critical review of the initial notion of an evolutionary development process based on the Western model has major policy implications. It has increasingly become politically correct to believe that efforts should no longer focus on formalizing the labour system. By way of an explanation for the essential reversal of the previous development trajectory, the suggestion now is that the privileges enjoyed by an exceedingly small proportion of the working population must end. The protection enjoyed by the elite within the workforce - who in Third World countries represent no more than a tenth of the total population living on the fruits of its labour power - is detrimental, according to this argument, to the efforts of the vast majority to improve the conditions in which they live. This 'unfair' competition could be avoided by abolishing security of employment, minimum wages and maximum working days, and numerous other labour rights which used to apply in the formal sector. But should we not then worry that things will get even worse for the quality of the labouring existence? No, those who call for flexibility to give employers a free hand to hire and fire as they please suggest that this approach would actually lead to more, and better work, and a rise in wages in real terms.

I myself have conducted several empirical case studies of the progress and impact of the informalization process in recent years. After the Asian economic crisis broke in mid-1997, I was able to observe its impact on work and welfare during a visit to Jakarta that autumn. Both national and international policy makers responded to the loss of jobs in the formal sector of the urban economy by suggesting that these workers who were 'temporarily' superfluous would easily find other work in the informal sector. The extent to which this was based on wishful thinking became clear when, between 1998 and 2000, I and an Indonesian colleague did research in rural Java on the impact of the loss of urban employment and the income it provided for a considerable proportion of the workforce in the two village where we located our investigations (Nreman & Wiradi, 202). Recently I undertook another study on the loss of jobs in the formal sector in the West Indian city of Ahmedabad. The closure of more than fifty large textile mills meant that, from the early 1980s on, some 1,00,000 to 1,25,000 factory workers lost their jobs. Based on anthropological fieldwork in the mill localities where they resided, I studied how their households fared after they were forced to join the informal sector (Breman, 2001, 2002). My findings unmistakably show deterioration in the living standards of the many workers who were no longer covered by the regulations applying in the formal sector.

The results of my research in Ahmedabad must be viewed in the light of the fundamental change in the labour policies of the Indian government. This turnaround came about not least because of pressure from multilateral agencies like the World Bank and the IMF. The idea that efforts should no longer be focused on increasing formalization of the labour system appears to have gained the status of political correctness. Analyses focusing on the positive side of the regime of economic informality are designed to ignore or explicitly reject the idea that anyone leaving the formal sector and joining the informal sector will automatically experience deterioration in their standard of living. This is based largely on the argument that working on one's own account and a one's own risk is that best route to development. The voluntary transfer suggested here is an option that very few of the former mill-hands in Ahmedabad, or the sacked formal sector workers in Jakarta, would support. As I have already explained, the choice was not theirs. It was forced mobility, and downward mobility at that. As soon as they lost their jobs, they realized that their lives were set to become much worse.

The Fallacy of Parallel Development

A paradigm which has dominated post-colonial development literature in the second half of the twentieth century suggested inclusion as a historical trend encompassing more and more people in different parts of the world. This particular brand of wishful thinking suggested that the process of transformation, as it had taken place in Western economies, would be repeated at the global level and in the end would give shape to the kind of industrial-urban society that had initially emerged on both sides of the Atlantic Ocean in the northern hemisphere. No doubt that historic trajectory had been difficult to predict when it first got started. Towards the end of the nineteenth century, there were strong doubt that the under classes in western societies would be able to accommodate themselves in the new industrial society that was being constructed. The doctrine of Social Darwinism was based on the assumption that not all poor people could or, for that matter, should be raised to a life of human dignity. In the struggle for survival only the fittest in the process of natural selection would be able to qualify themselves for a better future. As against the deserving poor, kept in waiting as a reserve army of labour, the non-deserving poor were labeled as a burden to themselves and to society at large. This sizable segment of the poor was blamed for their own poverty. Having nothing useful to add, their very presence was considered a risk to social stability and cohesion.

The subsequent inclusion of these marginalized people also in mainstream society was the outcome of a highly labour-intensive process of industrialization. The low level of technology, although rapidly increasing, allowed for the insertion into the workforce of households pushed out of the agrarian-rural economy. What became rephrased as the social question, conditioned on the one hand by growing assertiveness from below and on the other hand acceptance among higher classes that the cost of exclusion might be higher than inclusion, had its origin in an expanding economy, which required the labour power of the masses living in poverty. There is no clear indication that this development scenario which took place within the framework of the nation state is a century later replicated at the transnational level. On the contrary, the enormous gap between non-poor and poor people is still widening. This trend seems to have accelerated since the era of late-colonialism which was a major new round in the ongoing process of globalization. The Indian sociologist Andre Beteille has argued that no major civilization has ever fully excluded a concern for equality and that inequality has remained a feature also of modern society. He comments in this connection on the disjointed dynamics at the national and transnational level. 'I draw attention to the paradox that Western societies were acquiring a new and comprehensive commitment to equality of precisely that juncture in their history when they were developing in their fullest form the theory and practice of imperialism' (Beteille, 1983:4).

The assumption of parallel development explains why in the post-colonial era politicians and policy makers have gone on record saying that 'soon' or in 'the foreseeable future' people would no longer have to live in poverty. While they might have conceded that the fight against deprivation would take time and was dependent on all kinds of pre-conditions, they did not state that bringing increasing numbers and ultimately all people above 'the poverty line' was something that could not, or even should not, be contemplated. A well-known example of that mode of thinking was the idea of 'trickle down' which promised that people with few or no assets were eventually going to benefit from the process of economic growth. In line with the notion of inclusion as a historical trend, the British sociologist T.H. Marshall specified various dimensions of the process of inclusion and ranked them in a sequential order: first granting legal rights which extended the rule of low to all citizens, next the granting of political rights which proclaimed universal suffrage and promoted the participation of all in a democratic framework, finally the granting of socio-economic rights which found its apex in the welfare state (Marshall, 1975).

There have been episodes in the recent history of developed societies which seemed to signal that the trend towards inclusion can be abruptly halted or even reversed, i. e. a slide back into exclusion. The world economic recession in the 1930s exposed many people in the industrialized countries again to a situation of vulnerability which they found difficult to accept, precisely because of their improved wellbeing in the preceding decades. In 1933 a book was published, titled Die *Arbeitslosen von Marienthal.* It was an empirical study of the effects of long-term unemployment. The book became one of the classic works of social scientific literature on the significance of loss of paid employment for working-class households in an industrial society. The setting of the study was a small community on the outskirts of Vienna which has one large textile mill and not much else by way of economic activity. After cutbacks in production and working hours in the late 1920s, against the background of the economic crisis which affected the whole of industrial Europe, the mill closed in 1930. This meant the end of what was essentially the only source of employment in this rural township. With the complete workforce made redundant, no less than three-quarters of the local population, 367 of the 478 households, found themselves in a situation of acute and stark poverty. In summing up their findings the authors spoke of *Die mude Gesellschaft* (The Third Community). This subtitle to their study expressed the feelings of powerlessness and hopelessness that overwhelmed these people. Only a small proportion of the population managed to stay in paid work, in the service sectors outside the village, and a number of older people received pension. The study describes the response of the affected households in subsequent phases: how they proceeded from initial resolve to resignation, going on to despair and finally apathy. The social psychological approach illustrates how these people lost their sense of time and how the daily routine, which is so important for a meaningful life, was eroded. Outside the household, there was a noticeable increase in isolation, a declining involvement in the world outside, institutionally and organizationally, together with symptoms of envy and suspicion instead of mutual help. The tenor is clear: a process of marginalization, a shrinking of the psychological space, leading to alienation. The portrait demonstrates how tempting it is to hold the poor themselves accountable and responsible for the state of exclusion in which they are made to live.

How did the dismissed Austrian workers survive in those years of crisis? Certainly not through being above to find paid employment but by partially retreating into-self-sufficiency. They grew vegetables or bred rabbits on a small piece of land rented to them by the mill or the local council. Much more important than these modest contributions towards imposed autarky, however, was the state unemployment benefit which they received every fortnight. The economic cycle of the households affected by the mill closure revolved around this paltry payout. The benefits were funded from contributions by employers, workers and the local authority and the total accumulated in the years leading up to the closure meant that there were enough funds to last for 20 or 30 weeks. After that, the former mill workers were eligible for the lower benefits provided by a government dole. Sporadically, such as on religious holidays, the municipality or charity organizations would come with food packages. In the early 1930s the welfare state in Europe was still under construction. It would not be expanded and completed until well after the end of the Second World War, but the foundations had already been laid in the early years of the twentieth century. When the economic crisis struck in the early 1930s, governments in the industrialized part of the world responded to the sudden oneself of unemployment and impoverishment with relief programmes. These took the form of both financial support and job creation by commissioning public works. It is precisely this kind of public schemes which, in the free market-driven policies towards the end of the twentieth century, have been lacking or soft-pedaled in the global fight against poverty.

The essence of my argument in the pages above has been that past experiences are relevant for defining, analyzing and solving the dynamics of inclusion-exclusion in what is called the developing world. To promote incorporation into mainstream society and to forestall a return with a vengeance of the doctrine of Social Darwinism in the globalized economy, the deeply skewed balance between capital and labour will have to be redressed. Such a corrective policy needs to be carried out at the transnational, national as well as local level and requires (a) capital redistribution (land reforms in the first place); (b) employment creation and job security and (c) the provision of social welfare, concretized in terms of health, housing and education.

The huge disparities that have been created in today's world cannot be undone without connecting the mechanisms of inclusion to those of exclusion. As, for example, Seabrook has argued, it seems to be the object of official political discourse to suppress any such connections. 'The easiest alibi, as always, is to blame "nature", drought, over-population, the spread of the desert; when it is our own nature that is deeply implicated, above all in the nature of our society and its development, which has succeeded in re-creating a lasting sense of impoverishment out of the very riches it has accumulated, and has made us believe that the simple goal of sufficiency for all, represents for us the rich, not emancipation, but a terrifying loss not to be contemplated.' (Seabrook, 1985: 175)

References

1. Beteille, A., *The Idea of Natural Inequality and Other Essays*, Oxford University Press, New Delhi, 1983.
2. Breman, J., *Footloose Labour, Working in India's Informal Economy,* Cambridge University Press, Cambridge, 1996.
3. --------, *A Turn for the Worse; The Closure of the Ahmedabad Textile Mills and the Retrenchment of the Workforce.* The Wertheim Lecture 2001. Amsterdam School of Social Science Research, University of Amsterdam 2001.
4. -------, *The Labouring Poor in India: Patterns Of Exploitation, Subordination and Exclusion.* Oxford University Press, New Delhi, 2002.
5. G.Wiradi, *Good Times and Bad Times in Rural Java,* KITLV Press, Leiden 2001.
6. Jahoda, M., P. Lazarsfeld and H. Zeisel, *Die Arbeitslosen von Marienthal* (The Unemployed of Marienthal), Leipzig, 1933.

7. Marshall, T.H., *Social Policy in the Twentieth Century,* Hutchinson (4th rev. edition), London, 1975.
8. Seabrook, J., *Landscapes of Poverty*, Basil Blackwell, London, 1985.
9. Swaan, A. de, *In Care of the State; Health Care, Education and Welfare in Europe and the USA in the Modern Era,* Polity Press, Cambridge, 1988.
10. Wallerstein, I., "Globalization and the Age of Transition; a Long-Term View of the Trajectory of the World System, in: *International Sociology,* 15/2, 2000.
11. World Development Report 1995, *Workers in an Integrating World.* The World Bank, Washington, Oxford University Press, 1995, New York.

Globalisation, Justice and Development

Kamal Nayan Kabra

Every age tries to define itself. It defines itself with such aplomb, self-righteousness and self-indulgence as may make it apart from the reality by a big margin and outdo similar earlier attempts. They are powerful and telling examples of the power of language in the service of specific interests and objectives. The hegemonic power centers are likely to be endowed with notably sharp proclivity to be hyperbolic for a variety of material and socio-psychological reasons. Apart from helping them to win widespread legitimacy and help manage their operations without undue hiccups, such characterizations are used for distinguishing the present from the past and for showcasing it as a distinct improvement contributed by those who are steering the course of development. Such self-definitions may be couched in terms of either an accentuation or extension of some trends already underway or may represent a sharp break from the prevailing situation. The element of apotheosis in such characterization fulfils some functional as well as ideological roles. Particularly in situations when the stability and sustainability of the emerging order are contested and face actual or potential threats to their existence, the characterization is given multifarious, emotive, vague and opaque connotations in order partly to camouflage the real meaning and implications of the way things are organized and managed and partly to use it as an ideological weapon against the opposing forces. Thus it often happens that the overall characterizations of the dominant or desired trends add directions of emerging developments, even amounting to perpetration of neologisms, become highly controversial. It no longer remains clear whether they are shorthand, concise description of reality, or such a mixture of reality, value judgments, advocacy of certain lines of policy and action and implicit denunciation of the real and imagined opposition and counteracting forces, or an amalgam of these all. Little wonder that many different interpretations of the term appear to be simultaneously valid and operationally relevant.

Globalization: Beginning of the Story

It can be said that the above formulations seem to apply to the present-day buzz word 'globalization' in no small measure. The beginning of the 1970s saw the end of the post-Second War golden era of world-wide capitalist industrial growth. This period's high growth rates under conditions of near full employment and liberal rewarding of the working class in the rich countries was experienced in the wake of the new world order under the aegis of the Breton Woods arrangements. Certain other factors like the Keynesian macro-economic management, the super-power rivalry based Cold War which restrained the unhindered pursuit of narrow national commercial interests by the major trading and financial powers of the world, the growing clout of the trade unions, and the success in making the Third World, the growing clout of the trade unions, and the success in making the Third World adopt the catching-up mimetic industrialization as their very own agenda of development too contributed their bit to the high noon of world capitalism. The end of the golden era coincided with the collapse of the on-going attempts to reconcile modern, post-War capitalism with the interests and aspirations of the larger civic society, especially the domestic numerically large social groups like the industrial workers in the early industrialized, rich countries. Much before the existing socialism fell to pieces towards the end of the 1980s, there occurred the unceremonious disintegration of the welfare, social, regulated capitalisms in the advanced industrialized nations under the onslaught of the Thatcher-Reagan backlash. This extreme, one-sided pursuit of their sectional agenda by the dominant groups and classes in the North went a long way to make the general public believe the neo-classical resurgence in ideology, policy underpinnings and restructuring of the international economic relations as the only viable, historically proven option. With both the attempts to either reform or replace the capitalism world order meeting their waterloo, the neo-classical philosophy and policy regime labeled globalization seems to be enjoying a free run. Those who link up the present phase of what they christen as globalization, tend to make too much of the death and demise of Soviet socialism and that of its satellites. They forget that within their own societies a great change of equally, if not of more, momentous proportions took place in the form of the end of the liberal, social democratic and accommodative market system. This coincided with the counter-revolution in development theory and policy and the beginning of the era of structural adjustment in the image and along the lines of the Washington Consensus. It seems at this stage, a new phase began on the world scene. In order to capture and glorify this change, a relatively obscure and undefined term globalization started making rounds in popular writings, public discussions as well as policy councils and academic discourse no less than in many raging controversies in social sciences. The emerging age and its apostles, its commanding forces and interested and disinterested advocates gave themselves and their pursuits, goals, values and dream a name: globalization. Even since then, in a fairly explicit manner and from the very outset with a rather torrential speed, it was taken to be the name of what all is happening as also the direction, destination as well as the motor power and means for getting there, the globalized world. Its power and theoretical foundations and philosophical justification were taken of the history and promptly was declared to be irreversible as also something for which, it was claimed, 'there is no alternative'.

The information, communications, electronic and media revolutions were counted among the wellsprings of, or to be precise, were the technological enabling factors leading to globalization. Interestingly, these very 'revolutions' were pressed in to the service of globalization for portraying and propagating it as the supreme reigning reality of our time, and the inescapable destiny and *summum bonum* of the world. Thus, an all-embracing category has been found which is believed to have won open or tacit support of many groups and classes. This is the result of the all-pervading hegemony of the rich countries and their ruling/dominant elite. Globalization has been lapped up by the dominant and powerful ones, spread across nearly all continents, countries and cultures, who have managed to make it acceptable, with or without reservations, with or without common, shared understanding and a broadly comparable degree of commitment. Even those who would be at the receiving end of these processes of globalization have been globalized, that is, at least for the present. Whether in support of it, or in opposition to it, whether as active and predominant beneficiaries of it or its vocal or silent victims, globalization as the dominant theme of the current global concerns has come to acquire an unprecedented wide currency and central place in the public sphere. It covers fields as diverse as diplomacy or demography, religion or celebrity gossip, ecology or ethnography or entertainment, consumerist indulgence or conservationist moderation, technography leapfrogging and imitation or clinging to primordial identities. If brief, name what you will, it is made to relate to variously understood globalization. Not only the mundane humdrum of daily existence, but even the subtle and sublime creative arts, culture and literature, which had their strong local roots in the lives, living and, inner being and imagination of the masses and had strong localism as their characteristic forte from which spring the deep universal meanings and durability of these endeavours, are today humming the tunes of globalization; may be with heavy and irrecoverable cots, may be in a state of semi-conscious stupor, but as hard facts of life nevertheless.

Globalization penetrates the inner essence, motivation and actual operation of national and international politics. With its strong centralization in the economic, political, military and informational fields, paradoxically, it is supposed to be consistent with the somewhat divergent trends towards more effective federalization and decentralization of politics, giving credence to the quip: think global, act local in the interest of good governance. What is often described as a unipolar world is also portrayed by some to be an essential ingredient of globalization. However, the putative spread of democracy across countries and the pursuit of democratization of the international institutions, whether inner-governmental or related to international business or that arising from the emerging global civil society institutions, are also often supposed to be consistent with the creed of globalization. In brief, globalization is among those unique terms which do not have any unique meaning. It is made to encompass a great deal of diversity, differences, antagonistic elements and lack of clarity. Little wonder, it forms a part and parcel of the contemporary and historical inquiries as a real portmanteau category which cuts across paradigms, disciplines layers and forms of reality, and sharply polarized real, palpable interests and derision by a whole array of institutions and agencies standing in diametrically opposing, combatant positions. These uncomfortable and confusing aspects of the wildly popular concept of globalization appear to be both its positive and negative strengths, giving rise to the irony that it does not disappear from academic and practical discourse, because even in the face of these infirmities and oddities, the debates around it remain both light-bearing and fruit-bearing.

The power, sweep and influence of globalization are there for everyone to see and experience. It is certainly true that the market fundamentalists make use of globalization for their partisan ends. But to dismiss it as a myth and a figment of the imagination of the market fundamentalists may be as a reincarnation of some age-old phenomenon, would amount to an ostrich-like refusal to accept globalization as an objective thought-real which is incredibly influential and is capable of diverse interpretations.

One need not dwell more on the inchoate, diffused and partisan character of globalization. On the basis of the foregoing, it may be reasonable to infer that there is something about globalization which enables it to hold a centre stage position. This is so notwithstanding the fact that it is such a complex, multifaceted, vague, opaque, multi-disciplinary concept; that it is mired in the thick of controversies and refers at one and the same time to some major aspects of the putative and extant reality, ideas, policy ensemble as an instrument of ideological mobilization, centre point of advocacy, derision and denunciation of a particular world-view and solid manifestation of the interests and hegemony of certain forces at the apex of the world's economic, political, military and so-called cultural might. One may simply allude to a variety of alternative ways in which the reality and ideas coming under the rubric of globalization have been captured by any analysts by using a number of synonyms. These include corporate capitalism, capitalist world system, neo-liberalism, decolonization, transnational capitalism, market fundamentalism, globalism, totalitarian market order, neo-imperialism, free market world, global free market integration, Americanism, hegemony of the USA, North-centric and South-centric globalization, free and intensified global exchange of ideas, universal brotherhood in the style of Vasudhaiva Kutumbakam, etc. Evidently, the term "globalization" cannot unequivocally and simultaneously convey what all these different but inter-connected terms mean to convey. One wonders whether such vagueness is deliberate and is a factor behind its popularity. What is material is that an analysis of the processes, forces, impact and counter mobilization against globalization can take one around a conducted tour of the major contemporary issues, especially if one is interested in the fate of development of the Third World in its external and internal dynamics and what happens to the lofty ideals of enlightenment like democracy, justice, peace, solidarity and widely shared prosperity.

II

Neo-Liberal Foundatins: Facts and Fiction

To understand the phenomenon of globalization, we shall devote some attention to the foundations on which the concept stands. On this basis we proceed to analyze the forces, processes and real-life effects produced by it. We make use of two yardsticks, one of ensuring national development of the present day weak, poor and exploited countries, and the other of social justice for those against whom the prevailing social order incessantly operates for the purpose. A common thread seen across all the diverse concepts of globalization is the large-scale, growing and unhindered free flow of resources, goods and services, ideals, natural and legal persons, financial claims in the form of various old and new instruments characteristic of the present-day corpulent and predominant financial sector across national boundaries, whether in fact or as preferred courses at the level of policy permitted options. Thus, is appears that the essence of globalization is a borderless world - virtual global village. In this concept, clearly the unit of analysis is, of course, the nation-state. But at the ground level, the preponderate proportion of activities which constitute international economic relations do not have the nations as the operative, directly decision-making units. All these formerly controlled and regulated and now under globalization free cross-border activities are the activities of either natural or legal persons, who are the primary entities making decisions and, therefore, gaining or losing from them. True, the nation-state provides the legal and policy framework for these activities the same way as it does for the domestic activities except for the complications arising from separate national origins of the entities involved. Thus, the nation state enters the picture for determining the external sector policies and procedures, while the operational, micro decision-making entities are the natural and legal persons. Apparently, this mismatch has not emerged accidentally and has identifiable implications.

Multinational Enterprises and Globalization

For quite some time now, there is a growing realization of the attempts to make sense of the phenomenon called globalization to zero-in on the activities, role and behaviour of the large multinational enterprises (MNEs) who despite their size, power and close intertwining with the state, do not, mercifully, by themselves constitute the state. The large, multi-unit, multi-location vertically integrated common ownership and control MNEs are involved in high international transactions, including those between their subsidiaries and the principal and between the subsidiaries, which are, by definition, internal to them and hence cannot be treated as market transactions in any sense of the term. These intra-MNE transactions are not governed by the laws of demand and supply. How the so-called free international trade, the very soul and heart of the neo-liberal concept of globalization, can be treated as free, market-determined and unregulated when the intra-MNE, non-market exchange or transfer, decided by the management of the MNEs have become a very large part of the world trade, remains a rarely asked question.

An overwhelming proportion of the activities of the MNEs are confined to the rich countries, say the OECD countries, but the gospel of globalization proceeds as though it is the nation's and the national perspectives, needs and motivation and control over resources and capabilities which determine the course of those economic activities which cross- national boundaries without any hindrance by the nation states! The growing tendency is towards the formation of regional economic co-operation groupings, like the EU, NAFTA, etc. which account for as much as 70 per cent of international trade. They are relatively more integrated compared to the rest of the world and tend to have common international policies. This factor goes to detract from the hypothesis of market-led, all-encompassing global integration in a big way in so far as it is regionalization and not globalization which has acquired prominence. The evidence regarding persistence of price disparities beyond the transport costs and staggering income differentials flying in the face of factor price equalization in a globalized world with market-determined economic decisions are too uncomfortable facts for the neo-classical diehards who generally seem to be believing that if the world does not function according to their theoretical understanding, it must be a distortion, if not worse.

Thus, the conceptual basis of globalization seems to be erring on two counts. First, it takes the nation-states to be the players in the borderless world, while the actual players are a variety of natural and legal persons, who function under the legal framework of the nation states. Second, the whole exercise assumes of market-mediated cross-border economic contacts. But the fact is that the MNEs are the major players on the international arena who carry out a substantial part of their activities crossing international boundaries as non-market internal, intra-firm transactions. Moreover, most of these transactions take place among the entities belonging to the OECD countries, many of them tied together under regional groupings. Why does such a gross oversimplification and misrepresentation enter the concept of globalization? Probably, a line of inquiry can be found in the following formulation advanced by Noam Chomsky: 'The fantasy that the nations are the actors in the international arena is the standard doctrinal camouflage for the fact that within the rich nations, as within the hungry ones, there are radical differences in privilege and power (World Orders, Old and

New, 1994, 5). By taking the nations as the operative units operating on the global scene, the myth of 'free' exchange among sovereign, equal nations are sought to be given at least some formal validity, because the disparities between the entities within the nations are a bit too glaring and without any juridical fig leaf to be sustained even for a moment.

The fact of the matter is that it is no less a fiction that all independent, sovereign nations are equal and inter-relate on an equal footing in the global supermarket. Thus, even in its oversimplified garb, globalization understood as another name for the borderless world, is inherently asymmetrical. It seems to be inevitable that the world, as it stands today, at the end of its historical evolution, has become increasingly asymmetrical. Nothing has happened or has been done to undo the inherited and on-going disempowerment and the resulting agonies of the poor countries. The expected processes of convergence of the poorer countries as a result of following the industrialization, capital formation, technological up gradation path to development, as tried in the pioneer industrialized countries, have generally turned out to be counterproductive. Growing international and intra-national divergence and disparities may truly be regarded as the hallmark of the processes of international interaction as witnessed over the past five centuries or so.

Is East Asia an Exception?

The specially propped up relatively successful emulation by the East Asian newly industrialized countries is often cited as a living example of global socio-economic convergence. Apart from their sui generis, non-replicable special circumstances and favourable factors, they have turned out to be non-sustainable, excessively economistic and have extracted quite unconscionably high social, political, cultural and nationalistic costs from their citizens. The globalization of the East Asian tigers and their integration largely with the economies of the OECD countries followed in many ways a highly nationalistic course in the initial years, combining elements of import-substitution and export orientation (as a part of the strategy of the high labour cost economies of the North to use them as exclaves) along with capital controls (as concessional external borrowing went a long way to supplement their rather high domestic rate of savings) enforced by means of highly authoritative, undemocratic regimes surviving on the basis of the mighty presence of foreign armies on their soil, which along with many other factors, reduced them to the status of virtual semi-colonies.

Growing Asymmetries

The pertinent question is: are the asymmetries likely or expected to be reduced or enhanced because of the incipient or well-established processes of globalization? A positive answer is possible only by choosing to ignore the history of nation states and their interactions, especially over the last 500 years or so when the colonial rule, loot, one-way unilateral free trade and exploitation were rampant, and their lingering legacy persists in various forms even to this day. These processes and the resulting structures are made stronger using a number of subtle and not so-subtle devices, including most distressingly by means of making the former colonies fall prey, with the active collaboration of their modernizing elite, to the trap of catching-up, mimetic industrialization as the only effective means of opening the golden gates of progress and prosperity. The point is not that the modern science and technology should have been spurned lock, stock and barrel, as they are of foreign origin. That would be an absurd xenophobic proposition. The pertinent point to question is the blind imitation of the so-called advanced, industrialized nations without a critical examination of the feasibility and desirability of this path from the point of view of the needs, capabilities and aspirations of the poor and hungry toiling masses of the former colonies. Given the significance of the development experience of the North, the fact of vastly different domestic conditions and qualitatively changed character of the global conjuncture facing the poor countries, a critical and people-centric examination of the development challenges would surely suggest significant departures from the European and North American path. The vested interest of the North to perpetuate dependence of the late arriving nations have led them lately to devise a new instrument in the form of the WTO. How the same old game has been played is best illustrated by the ridiculous and absurd way the connotation of trade has been broadened in the WTO agreement 'to include production, distributing, marketing, sale and delivery' (Shukla, S.P., 2002, 271) as though trade is synonymous with all the economic activities in general! In view of these factors, can one treat unregulated economic and other inter-relations, called globalization a fair, equitable and effective policy course for ensuring development?

The last few decades over which the present phase of globalization is supposed to have been in operation have seen worsening of the development reality and prospects. Similarly, the global line qualities, both between nations and among the various socio-economic groups within the nation all over the world have become disgustingly wider and sharper. The distressing facts on these issues are made widely known on a regular basis by the annual Human Development Reports of the UNDP and the World Development Reports of the World Bank, as also by numerous publications of the UNCTAD, ILO, etc. Many scholars have given a historical account of the intensifying global inequalities. The severity of the growing inequalities can be gauged by the fact that 'the 400 highest income earners in the United States make as much money in a year as the entire population of 20 African nations - more than 300 million people' (Robert Weissman, Multinational Monitor, July - August, 2003). The magnitude of the problem is reflected in the following passage: "Global Inequalities persist at staggering levels. The richest 10 per cent of the world population's income is roughly 117 times higher than the poorest 10 per cent, according to the calculations performed by the economists at the Economic Policy Institute, using data from the International Monetary Fund. This is a huge jump from the ratio in 1980, when the income of the richest 10 per cent was about 79 times higher than the poorest 10 per cent. Excluding the fast growing China from the equation, the disparities are even more shocking. The income ratio from the richest 10 per cent to the poorest 10 per cent rose from 90: 1 in 1980 to 154 :1 in 1999' (*Ibid.*).

One can supplement these facts by those on poverty, food insecurity, malnutrition, incidence of morbidity and mortality, more specifically of infant mortality, illiteracy, unemployment, international indebtedness of the poor countries, the reverse and perverse transfer of financial resources from the poor to the rich nations, worsening terms of trade of the poor, primary goods exporting countries, violent volatility of financial flows to the poor, newly industrializing countries, growing fiscal impotence of the states, the iniquitous character of the WTO provisions, specifically its provisions regarding intellectual property rights, trade related investment measures, agricultural exports, trade in services and the further items on the negotiations block, called the Singapore issues (RIS: World Trade and Development Report, 2003). In addition to these glaring facts which provide but a fleeting glimpse of the deeply embedded inequalities as the hall mark of the present world order, made worse by the ever- increasing resource base and the resulting clout of the family controlled mega MNEs (about 80 per cent of them are under family control), the hyper growth and mind-boggling size of the international financial flows, mainly very short-run speculative, hot money flows, nearly totally unconnected to the real economy, tend to show the unjust and anti-development character of much of what is happening by way of global inter-relationships, specially the capital inflows from the large financial markets to the poor countries as the much trumpeted basis for initiating the processes of their convergence with the rich and industrialized countries. A new threat in the form of international crime syndicates has assumed menacing proportions as a result of the combination of domestic deregulation with global scale free play of the MNEs, motivated by the narrow financial calculus of their controlling families under the symbiotic protection of the political-administrative classes. Now that it has become clear that the expected trickle-down effects of the growth of GDP do not materialize even in the domestic economy, let alone on the global scale, even with the helping hand of the pull-up programmes and their international counterparts in the form of ODA and the so-called international development co-operation, it is rather native to expect that such convergence can become a reality via the operation of the trickle-down and spread effects across national boundaries.

Intertwining of the Internal and the External Factors

What needs to be specially underlined is that both external and internal peripheralization are closely interconnected. Peripheries have been defined as 'regions where conditions in the field of policies, economy, social structure, religion and ideology are organized in favour of people living in other regions' (Hands-Heinrich, Nolte, 2003, p.51). Obviously, colonial rule and the institutionalization of a similar process after the end of formal occupation, say, e.g. in the form of dependence of the poor countries on the early industrialized nations, rather on their large companies controlling the production of capital goods and their high level, sun-rise technologies, as also for meeting the critical shortfalls in savings and foreign exchange required for this kind of industrialization, contributed in a large measure to the processes of peripheralization of poor nations, regions and classes of people. This is how there emerged the well-known dependency syndrome. These processes and their outcomes gave the indigenous capitalist classes new opportunities for cementing their industrial and economic power within the domestic economic and political space, based on a love-hate relationship with the metropolitan MNEs. Similar processes are continuing under globalization, understood as a multifaceted, complex phenomenon related to the totality of international relations which has strong links with the internal power structure in every inter-linked, externally dominated country. This kind of dominance of the external factors can be seen even in the economies which are basically inward-oriented with a relatively small size of the external linkages. This is explicable mainly in terms of the strong impact of the historical legacy of post-colonial economic structures, the initial conditions and the strong-arm policies of the North for guiding their relationship with the Third World in order to serve their narrow, partisan, non-global objectives. The stylized facts and what we have just discussed on some limited aspects of global inequalities, mentioned earlier, show that the processes of centralization and concentration unleashed by the processes of capitalist industrialization in a high inter-linked framework in the Third World countries owe themselves in no mean measure to the domestic power structures as well.

To understand this relationship between the internal and external peripheralization vis-a-vis the core or metropolitan centres, it is useful to recall how this complex relationship has been brought out in a very telling, realistic and effective manner by Johan Galtung.

According to his analysis, 'the impact of the rich upon poor nations can best be understood if the global political economy is viewed as the relationship between a "centre"(the developed countries) and a "Periphery" (the less developed countries), each of which is further subdivided into its own

'centre' (the governing elite) and "periphery" (groups without much power of wealth)' (Mahler, V.A., 1999, 384). The pattern of their mutual interaction involves the exercise of power over these countries even after they attained their political independence not by so called multilateral agencies like the World Bank and its affiliates, the IMF, WTO, etc., but 'indirectly by means of a two stage process in which the centre of the Centre nation structures the option of the periphery of the Periphery nation itself' (Ibid.). Describing the working of this mechanism of exercising remote and indirect control by the North over the South based on the experience of Latin America, a scholar expands on the theory of Galtung. He maintains that in addition to the co-option and active utilization of the centre of the Periphery, the middle classes too become a part of the bridgehead of the centre of the Centre nations. He says, "The middle classes of Buenos Aires, Rio de Janeiro, and Santiago de Chile, who completely accept the European and North American standards of consumption....live about as well as, or better than the middle class persons who live in the advanced countries. But the poor of Brazil, Argentina and Chile are poor by the grim standards of the poor in Latin America' (Karl Deutsch quoted by Hans-Heinrich, op. cit. p. 385). It may be pointed out that none of these countries are isolated. Instead, they are rather closely 'integrated' with the economies of the North, more specifically with that of the USA.

To sum up , the incongruities and oddities contained in the concept of globalization as a result of taking nations as the relevant units, ignoring the internal entities and their interface with the global factors and the neglect of the historical legacy of large initial, inherited inequalities (leading to non-recognition of the many asymmetries and their implications for so-called free and unfettered global interaction networks) are not the only problems one would have with the exaggerated claims made regarding the real character and implications of globalization. The real entrepreneurs, the small formal and informal units, can hardly operate beyond the local level. This is so notwithstanding the much talked about flexible specialization and networking and the information and communications revolution, especially in view of the monopolization of the bulk of the socio-economic space by the giant MNEs and the relative resource poverty and weaker bargaining strength of the small formal and informal entities.

Moreover, in this view of globalization there is only some faint and fleeting recognition of the non-economic elements that force their way in the otherwise highly economistic perspective, like for instance in the form of calling attention to what is termed social capital. In fact, in the tradition of neo-liberalism which provides the foundations of the generally prevalent concept of globalization, the economy is taken to be what Karl Polanyi called a socially disembodied entity, i.e., a practically autonomous economy which exists and operates as though the other spheres of life hardly matter. This theoretical basis makes globalization nearly exclusively an economic phenomenon, economic ideology, economic policy package and an ensemble of all these. It is obvious that this is an artificial construction, an apologetic, ideological device which is not sustainable either on theoretical grounds or on the basis of the empirical evidence regarding the joint, non-separable functioning of the economy from the rest of the elements of society. As a corollary, globalization cannot remain confined merely to the economic domain. This is a very serious, meaningful, realistic and powerful re-discovery of globalization as it operates and at the normative level is sought to be popularized and imposed on the whole world. For facilitating an assessment of the meaning and implications of globalization for development and its inalienable component, justice, this re-discovery goes a long way. The point we intend to make on the basis of this discussion, therefore, is that the mechanics of globalization can hardly be appreciated unless the intra-national entities involved in the dealings with the entities in the other countries in many diverse spheres are brought into the picture, more particularly in order to see how globalization impacts the development of the poor countries and the nature and degree of justness of its mechanism and outcomes.

The fact nonetheless remains that predominantly as an economic category which operates in close association with the political and cultural processes, which are sought to be captured by the ideology termed "globalism" (Steger, 2002), and a neo-classical market-determined and dominated policy package, globalization is an objective, though partial and an age-old reality. It can be seen in the form of multifarious intensified direct and indirect relationships between the citizens of different countries. Tall claims are made by its protagonists about its capacity to provide solution to all the problems the world faces at large. They loudly proclaim its invincibility and irreversibility, as though it exhausts all the options which can be thought of or exist. It has managed to win the sanction and support of the powerful states, their MNEs, and most political formations either exercising political power or that are in close proximity to power centers in different parts of the world, as an accepted set of cure-all state policies in all the major countries. It has managed to become the darling of those who control and dominate the media, cultural outfits and other elite opinion-makers. It is true that many incisive, intellectually impressive, tightly argued and convincingly well documented political economy critiques of this brand of globalization have appeared in current social science. For instance, Manfred Steger (2002, 47-79) discusses the following five central claims made in order to sell globalization and show their vacuity:

1. Globalization is about the liberalization and global integration of (national) markets.
2. Globalization is inevitable and irreversible.
3. Nobody is in-charge of globalization, as though it is a natural, elemental and spontaneous development and being nobody's doing, like for example what Thomas Friedman calls the electronic herd and the global super market (The Lexus and the Olive Tree, 2000), nobody can be blamed for its selective and discriminatory effects.
4. Globalization benefits everyone which is possible only by assuming it to be based on symmetrical relationships or philanthropy on the part of those who are in a position to command the processes of international inter-connectedness.
5. Globalization furthers the spread of democracy in the world.

Based on many critiques of globalization in its different but inter-related connotation, the world is witnessing many widely networked, vocal, even militant and expanding ground level and joint international movements involving a growing number of global, national, local and mixed civil society institutions. The latter are stridently and doggedly exposing this brand of globalization for what it is by mass mobilization, especially of the growing army of those on whom a heavy load of miseries is regularly heaped upon by the relentless pursuit of its highly sectarian agenda. However, the forces of globalization continue to maintain their upper hand. This may be related to the close equation between the content of globalization and the interests of those who are controlling the commanding heights in the largest and most powerful countries of the world in economic, financial technological, political, cultural and ideological sphere. The resulting clout helps its protagonists to acquire a position of great influence in moulding public opinion and setting the agenda of the day. Moreover, there are some objective factors which either work or are deftly made to work in support of the neoliberalism-based globalization.

To make sense of these pro-globalization factors, one has to recognize that growing extensive and close inter-connectedness has become an incontrovertible fact of life across the globe. This has been facilitated to an unprecedented extent by the revolution in the means of transport, communication, information gathering, processing, storage and dissemination as also substantially easy and not too unaffordable access to these by at least the vast middle-income groups. The global inter-connectedness and close interaction are spread over many aspects of peoples lives, with both positive and negative implications. Among these, one may randomly make a mention of space, economy, life style and consumption patterns, cultural symbols, political participation, national and international travel, entertainment, migration, exposure to ecological and environmental crises, threat of nuclear annihilation, homogenization of aspiration and values, sway of crass individualism, decline of communitarian ethos and ethics, mass poverty and deprivation in the midst of the growth of super-high productive potential and its large-scale actualization in at least some countries. One can go on to add ever more items concerning which the whole world has shrunk, come closer and is facing shared challenges and opportunities. Of course, this is accompanied by grossly iniquitous sharing of the costs and benefits and a sharpening realization of the chasm between what could be available to people at large, and what is actually obtained by the thinly minority at the apex and the vast multitudes of people below. In this respect the neo-liberal publicists tend to give a highly exaggerated list of the matters in which the world has come closer together, implying as though the potential is also the real, and further that what has become available to some is going to become available to everyone at least to a modest extent only if these processes are allowed to continue for a reasonable but foreseeable length of time. Clearly the neo-liberal universe is highly exclusionary. According to their world view derived from Social Darwinism, those who fail to jump on to the globalization bandwagon do not ultimately matter and are socially dispensable.

It is also rarely factored in that continuous expansion of the spatial-geographical frontiers of mankind is an age-old process and the present phase is its latest phase, but certainly is far from being the humane, just, participatory and inclusionary with healthy concern for the environment and the future generations. Nor has we reached a stage to justly maintain that it is a tribute to the positive ambience generated by the world globalization that instead of discarding the present partisan and iniquitous globalization, alternatives are proposed as South-centric globalization or globalization from below.

Let us call attention to the multidimensional expansion of the network of human social interactions and increasingly wider spatial inter-connections which have been growing ab initio in order to see how the present globalization is similar to and/or different from similar earlier processes. The expansion of the society, polity and markets from the local to the regional to the national and to the global has taken many centuries but is yet to incorporate the majority as participants in the decision-making processes and consequently as their beneficiaries rather than remaining passive recipients of its mostly negative consequences as far as most of humanity is concerned. Such an extension has, moreover, not been consecutive but has moved on simultaneously and the wider levels of spatial linkages do not render the earlier narrower ones ineffective or unimportant. The emergence of the national does not, for instance, necessarily marginalize the regional and/or local. Similarly, despite the strides made by the international inter-connectedness, even in most non-autarchic countries, the local and intra-national linkages far outweigh the international linkages. This is correct even for the most powerful and industrialized rich countries championing globalization. Long- distance trade, setting up of empires spanning many continents, spread of religion and ideologies like wild fire across many countries and continents, financial transactions and movement of precious metals as medium of exchange as well as a storehouse of values between the residents of many countries, shifting of residence and habitats in the form of mass exodus, etc., are in effect, close cousins of what is presently projected as globalization. However, even if the global inter-connections and mutual dependence are not entirely new and fair, the subjective realization of this objective fact is far more widespread today than possibly ever before.

For a better part of history, the antecedents of global, cross-border multifaceted relationships were without governmental restrictions, though the cost and risk of giving effect to the long spatial movements were a formidable barrier. Apart from collecting entry/exit taxes, one has not seen any of the plethora of restrictive measures in the pre-capitalist era, except for the serfs under certain types of feudalism. It has often been pointed out that the extent of international inter-linkages among different nations from the initial years of the Industrial Revolution up to the First World War were, in fact, more than those seen after the 1970s. But the present public policy stance of permitting the growth of global linkages without undue restrictions (more by way of loud pronouncements and for adoption by others, while departing from these free norms in their national interest by the powerful countries at will in many open and dubious ways, rendering the claims regarding 'free' movement as hypocritical) is also not entirely new, though it stands in contrast with what was witnessed during the inter-war years and which continued to an extent right up to the early 1970s. In many ways the legacy of protectionism persists even after the WTO by the trading majors in many diverse ways.

Then what is so special about the globalization of the last few decades of the 20th century which is continuing with added gusto? The classic analysis of the capitalist development in the Marxist tradition has demonstrated the inherent tendency of internationalization of capitalist accumulation to which international movements of labour too contribute a great deal. Thus, neither in theory nor in actual conditions evolving in different countries, there is any of this out of the ordinary or unusual in so far as global economic, social, political and environmental interdependence is growing. The tendency was there; it has picked up speed or has been made to move faster and, of course, in the directions, like the financial assets and instruments, preferred by those who are in the commanding positions. After all, even the earlier big spurts in cross-border dealings owed a great deal to the dramatic technological advances of the respective periods. Not only that, the policy of free trade versus protectionism has all along been highly controversial. Then one wonders why is there so much song and drama about the present phase of largely public policy-induced freer and larger flow of goods and services, factors of production and daily financial claims of astronomical size along with diminished movement of natural persons. That the composition of the basket of tradable changes requires a different policy configuration to sustain itself is understandable. This happens because the leading sectors change, technological change acquires a different complexion and with higher incomes, changed distribution of income, wealth and social power and more pronounced role of the hidden persuaders, the composition of both demand and supply changes.

As maintained above, globalization is portrayed as much as a short and crisp name for the existing reality, though hardly as its *differentia specifica*, as also in order to capture the ideology behind it but by a soft, pleasant and non-offensive term which helps create a favourable ambience. It is considered useful in silencing and/ or confusing the critics and opponents. Capitalisms of different historical times and of different countries have been known variously as free economies, market economies, liberal- democratic countries, laissez faire systems, atomistic systems, etc. Their usage did not arouse so many and so intense debates and controversies as have greeted the characterization of the present phase of capitalism as *globalization*. Clearly, it is not the name, the term "globalization" which arouses so much passion, intellectual opposition and deep antagonism. What invokes opposition is the drive to push a highly sectarian policy package as a universally beneficial and desirable one.

Before we deal with this question, it may be helpful to try to understand the tactics adopted by the protagonists of globalization in order to protect their turf. This involves attempts to blunt the criticism against globalization by sidetracking the real issues and misrepresent the criticisms. Let us take one instance. It is certainly intellectual dishonesty to criticism the critics of globalization for being narrow-minded, like the frogs in a well, *koop mandooks*, as we in India say, or chauvinistic, who want to erect high walls around themselves in order to insulate themselves from the free flow of ideas from outside the walls they themselves have put up out of their sheer myopia or worse. No, not so much of humanity, from around the globe, including the *creme de la creme*, cutting across differences and diversity, and with the best of motives similar to any which have spawned enlightened movements in history, could have mobilized themselves in to concerted, multifaceted action if globalization were to mean free open and unhindered movement and contest of various views, theories, ideologies, scientific and technological knowledge.

In so far as the WTO brand of globalization is wedded to measures like Trade Related Intellectual Property Rights which also sanctifies the attempts by the MNEs to improperly appropriate the traditional knowledge systems of the indigenous peoples and their regional biodiversity, it is the protagonists of globalization who are putting up barriers against free flow of ideas as a part of their drive to forge global monopolies. Such mobilizations and intellectual ferments are an indication that having seen so much which is akin to the reality of global inter-connectedness and what-have-you as concrete-real in the past as well it is the ideological and policy content of the present wave of globalization and globalism which is inviting opposition. It is evident that globalization, as understood in the current discourse has nothing whatsoever to do with free flow and interchange of ideas, ideologies and policy debates. In fact, it is the votaries of globalization who deny and deride the existence of alternatives and pompously declare that with the collapse of the opposition to the US dominance of the world by a more or less equally powerful superpower and the ideology it claimed to uphold, the resulting unipolar world has become devoid of alternatives; according to them, it is the end of history! A serious exercise is called for in order to understand the vocal, well-meaning and intellectually powerful opposition to what is called globalization and the reasons for which and the devices by means of which it is sought to be imposed on the whole world as the only course available to it. As we proceed, we intend to show that it is the anti-development and anti-justice thrust of globalization, and the resulting insecurity and nervousness of the perpetrators of this unjust system, especially following the post-1970 slow-down of the major capitalist countries, among other factors, which are fueling the powerful anti-globalization movements across the globe. Truly, just as the term "globalization" has become globalized, so is the opposition to it truly global!

Is it possible that the pro-statist forces are opposing globalization as the pro-liberalization-globalization forces intend to roll back the state? This seems a facile and mistaken view. The controversy over the role of the state in the economic sphere arises from a historical, unrealistic, narrow and mistaken view of the economy as a socially disembodied entity because market exchange is considered the sole mechanism available for organizing and coordinating human social affairs. The moment the historical and contemporary facts regarding the simultaneous occurrence of and reliance on reciprocity, redistribution, house holding are recognized for social organization and motives other than the pursuit of material prosperity are treated as relevant for the social human beings, the state-market dichotomy and polar opposition fall in place and come out in their true colour. The issue then no more remains whether the state is active in the economy or withdraws or is reduced to a minimalist position. But the issue then is transmogrified into what kind of role the state plays, how and for whose benefit, at least predominantly if not entirely. Viewed in such a framework, one finds that the issue between the protagonists and antagonists of globalization is not whether the state participates in the economy, (which has invariably been the case), but whose game it would play, how and at what cost to various sections of society, i.e., who would yield the stick of state power to further economic interests and who would be made to foot the bill.

For one thing, none of the earlier phases emerged and survived without a powerful backing, even a catalytic role of the state. Karl Polanyi showed the emergence of laissez faire regimes, exploding the myth of self-regulated markets as the organizing mechanism of capitalist economies. Similarly, the states of the North, the international institutions they dominate and the academic establishment under their tutelage worked together to administer deadly blows to the state-regulated, reformist and welfare capitalism in Western Europe and North America with their stillborn social markets in order to make place for the present day supposedly market-ruled globalization. That is to say, globalization owes itself in no small measure to state's active role, though, of course, in a highly selective manner. The state activities which find favour with the globalists are those which facilitate and encourage cross border, unrestricted movements of goods, services and financial resources according to the preset economic needs of the rich, industrialized countries, mainly the G-7 countries and the big MNEs originating and controlled from them. Their shifting comparative advantage, the compulsions arising from the structural changes in their economies and their relative competitive position in the world economy determine the nature, extent and areas of free movements of goods and services and factors of production they require. For instance, when the productivity gains of the Newly Industrialized Economies of East Asia started posing a threat to the US, industry, and the services sector, mainly in R&D and the financial sector became the leading sectors of the US economy around mid-1970s, the whole game plan was changed in favour of what is presently known as globalization. In these changes the MNEs play a very active role in order to use the state power for moving ahead with their agenda. It may be clarified that the so-called multinational or transnational companies are very much the corporate citizens of their mother countries. The MNEs and their mother countries reinforce each other's power as a result of which global economic, social, political, cultural and military power has become heavily concentrated and centralized. The close symbiotic relationship between the global business corporations and their mother countries comes out quite vividly in the following view expressed by Thomas Friedman, the author of one of the best-sellers on globalization: 'The hidden hand of the market will never work without a hidden fist--the hidden fist that keeps the world safe for Silicon Valley's technologies is called the US Army, Air Force, Navy and Marine Corps' (Quoted by GIndin, Sam, 2002, p.8). It is for such reasons that Henry Kissinger described globalization as another name for the US domination of the world. It is this kind of exclusionary and asymmetric character of the present-day globalization which invokes growing resentment and opposition.

Even in the economic sphere, instead of the real economy, it is the financial sector with its astronomical size of daily cross border transactions (apparently the leading sector of the presently reigning globalization) which is the heart of the present-day globalization. These speculative, casino-like financial supermarkets are the play grounds of the rich, mainly the rich OECD countries, but with a very volatile and mercurial presence in some select poor but large economies. Everywhere these financial markets are dominated by the electronic herd (i.e. 'millions of investors moving money around the world with the click of a mouse' like 'faceless stock, bond and currency traders sitting behind computer screens all over the globe moving their money around from mutual funds to pension funds to emerging market fund, or trading on the Internet from their basements' (Thomas Friedman, pp.13 and 109). It is mammon-worship by these speculators who could not care less about the real economic implications of their games.

The dominant economic activity of the present-day globalized world takes place in the financial sector (where mega profits of the MNEs too are parked and deployed). As a concomitant of this feature, the rule of the real economy and, as business entities, unconcerned with the fate of the real toiling human beings spread over the shrunk global village, too has become secondary to that of the speculative electronic herds largely operating in the secondary stock markets. These casinos generate by their daily transactions worth trillions of dollars, huge flows of income and stocks of wealth without producing an extra blade of grass or additional employment in the farms and factories anywhere, including for the periphery of the Centre. In fact, the threat of moving their capital and enterprises around in the search for cheaper sources of inputs, including labour becomes a weapon in the arsenal of big business to impose compliance on the working classes. On the contrary, this diversion of potentially productive resources from the real to the financial sector and concentrated in ever fewer hands restricts the growth of demand for wage-goods and other goods and services capable of enhancing the quality of life for the deprived majority of humanity in remote godforsaken regions of the world. The state- supported control over the R & D industry in the hands of the MNEs has a bias against encouraging labour use and goes to build technological bias against employment expansion, not to speak of the environment- hostile and culturally depraved lifestyle and values fostered by them. To the extent, new technologies lead to the introduction of new products with heavy draft on energy and natural resources and belong to very high price ranges beyond the reach of the vast majority; they lead to pollution, exclusion and social discontent. In this information age and a shrunk world, the victims of the financial market volatility, super unearned financial gains neither know who are wreaking havoc on their lives and living nor are in a position to find out the sources from which these thunderbolts strike them with erratic regularity.

It would be too much for the present to give an exhaustive treatment to the subject to show how sectarian, narrowly focused, exclusionary and unjust the present processes of North-centric globalization are. What has been briefly examined is enough to show what is its essential thrust and why. The controversies surrounding the popular concept of globalization can be attributed to its working and results. These negative features represent an intensification of the normally obtainable unjust effects of a capitalist economy but with the abolition of its welfare and social security measures and the replacement of Keynesian approach towards fuller employment by labour market flexibility, meaning in simple words, sacrificing the welfare and rights of labour on the altar of the profits of the big business. The unsung and unwept liquidation of the reformist structural and policy initiatives by the triumphalism of the Reagan-Thatcher Anglo-American counter-revolution has made the sea rough and stormy for the smooth sailing of globalization.

III

Globalization and Development

Let us give some specific attention to the impact of the presently existing globalization on the processes and prospects of development of the Third World. In this entire analysis, one has to sharply distinguish the present phase of globalization with the earlier periods when similar internationalism trends and relationships, elements of a veritable international economic system, were no less visible. As Polanyi has said with reference to the last quarter of the 19th century, 'Only a madman would have doubted that the international economic system was the axis of the material existence of the human race.' But during that period, these international linkages were not picked up for defining the essential character of the time, nor went to the extent of denying the presence of alternatives. The 19th century globalization imposed itself on the Third World in the form of a long period of imperialist rule and contributed in a major way to the disempowerment of these countries leading to a high degree of internal disarticulation and disparity. Is the present late 20th century-early 21st century globalization qualitatively different from its predecessor and likely to produce a different kind of outcome? It would apparently be reasonable to expect a different kind of outcome from the present phase and form of globalization in view of the fact that the Third World has wrested political independence, is consciously pursuing the path of progress with the active support and under the guidance of the former colonial masters and is supposed to be enjoying the 'advantage' of late start. This putative advantage is supposed to arise from the view which suggests that the late-late-late industrializes do not have to reinvent the wheel and can fall back upon not only the lessons the early developers learnt at the school of hard knocks but can also count upon the physical, technological and financial resources of the rich countries with whom the poor countries now can relate as sovereign nations. The first flush enthusiasm and bonhomie regarding the co-operative pursuit of developing the laggard regions could not last beyond the 1970s when both the groups of countries that were supposed to be working as "partners in progress" reached an impasse. The attempts at architecting a "New International Economic Order" (NIEO) by the Third World were related to the enthusiasm generated by the success of the OPEC countries to raise the oil prices. The NIEO was intended to increase the space available to the poor countries and correcting some of the inequities they were made to suffer. But it came to nothing. In fact, these exercises met their denouement in the form of the supposed helplessness of dozens of Third World countries to accept the structural adjustment programme (SAP). In a way, the SAP replaced the stillborn NIEO.

The SAP, consisting mainly of liberalization, privatization and globalization (LPG), is the face of the present era of globalization the Third World has been confronted with as the new development policy they are coaxed, coerced and cajoled to adopt. Once again this time around too the development tool kit for the Third World has been manufactured, packed, shipped and sold to the poor countries by the intellectual workshops of the world located in the G-7 countries, mainly the USA with active collaboration by the comprador intellect workers of the poor countries. One purpose for which it was designed and handed down to the debt-ridden poor countries was to integrate them, covetously christened "emerging markets", with the economies of the rich countries who happen to be their main trading partners (what with weak or practically non-existent South-South relations) and suppliers of capital in various forms to meet their savings, foreign exchange and technology gaps. The other was to speed up their rate of growth by freeing them from the unsuccessful statist growth-retarding policy and planning trap and the associated democratic portfolio funds by rather "sexist" make-up of their external face, and open-arm welcome of foreign capital by giving them as national treatment as given to deregulated domestic capital (considered the key elements for keeping the confidence level of the electronic herd high as reflected in the country credit-rating by basically mercenary credit-rating agencies) were considered effective enough for attaining market determined high speed and efficient growth. To mask these growth fundamentalist policies with a 'human face' as a politically correct framework for implementing, the new globalization package without injuring the fragile electoral democracies, having a rather high degree of manageability of the popular verdict by the resourceful, it was thought that the poor and deprived were to be taken on board by a combination of trickle-down effects supplemented by liberally funded pull-up programmes. This latter course of action, otherwise burdensome in view of the fiscal crunch, was to be made feasible by the supply side response of a low tax rate regime.

This SAP- based development intervention by the globalized regime can be examined either in the light of the outcomes seen over the last two decades or on an *a priori* basis. As far as the former approach is concerned, so much negative evidence from across the world has accumulated that the originators of the Washington Consensus, who fathered the SAP, have come out with disclaimers to the effect that they did not say so, or that they were misunderstood. No country in the Third World has come out with flying colours even with respect to the growth fundamentalist sectional agenda. So many miracle economies of yesteryears seem to have ended up not with a bang but with a whimper. One thing is clear. The structure, institutional ensemble and global equations of the Third World needed a thorough re-doing along with the introduction of a series of positive policies and programmes on the basis of internal regeneration, reassessment ad restructuring rather than superimposition of a mimetic, catching-up agenda with continued dependence and asymmetric relationship with the rich world and the absence of meaningful and substantial mutual co-operation among the poor and disempowered countries. Both the earlier economics of development and the later- day counter-revolution in development economics and the interventions based on them fail to recognize that the growth of a diseased structure cannot lead to the emergence of a healthy system, unless correctives to remove the malignancy, malfunctioning and malaise are undertaken at least simultaneously. Despite wide-ranging socio-economic changes, expansion, diversification, role and place in the world economy, introduction and applications of many advances and fruits of science and technology, expansion of modern socio-economic infrastructure facilities on a scale not seen before, establishment of many new institutions of 'modernization', etc., in most of the Third World countries, a multi-dimensional crisis has engulfed most of the Third World countries in varying proportions. The crisis has become acute in so far as it is becoming increasingly intractable by the application of the battery of conventional measures of more of the same variety, even though with changed composition. True, there has taken place a sizeable increase in the absolute number of those who have derived net benefit in conventional terms from the process of economic expansion; they live longer and their consumption of goods and both public and private services is higher and more varied than even before, though not necessarily in more secure and eco-friendly environment and possibly with more acute psychological disquietude. But the number of those who do not have livelihood security, and in one word, are made to bear a disproportionately large burden of the costs and negligible share of its benefits and in many cases remain uninvited to the high table of development, is not only uncomfortably large and growing, but is threatening the sustainability of such partisan, partial and unjust growth. It remains unsustainable not only owing to the ecological disturbance and heavy costs but because of the growing disjunction between various aspects of social existence at macro and micro levels both within the nations and internationally.

In short, the intentional endeavours for development under the present package of globalization policies, which are in many ways a continuation of the statist development policies but with a more open adoption of market and capital-friendly policy instruments (made respectable by the state failure to withstand the onslaught by the market forces), remain incomplete, unbalanced, iniquitous and mimetic rather than based on a real exercise of internally evolved choices in an open, democratic set of social relations capable of overcoming the pangs and costs of centuries- old disempowerment which was imposed on large sections of humanity in the most inhuman manner. That even substantial and sustained rate of growth of national income remains an unrealized dream by most of the Third World countries shows the inappropriate foundations and policy design derived from the SAP. Whether the free and open-door policies based current phase of globalization under the corporatist framework or the earlier statist forms of attempts to link up with the advance industrialized economies in order to catch-up with them on improved terms compared to the legacy of colonial domination, the essential difference was mainly with respect to the choice of the instruments and policies and not concerning the substance and content of 'development'.

It has been argued that the SAP is basically designed to inspire the confidence of the international financial markets in the safety and profitability of their financial resources made available to the poor economies in various forms as also for ensuring sustained growth of demand for the fast accumulating vast financial resources of the investors from the rich countries, additionally supplemented now by the reverse inflow from the poor to the rich countries and their on-going recycling (Bienefeld, M. 1993). The manner in which, despite the rapidly growing external indebtedness and yawning and expanding trade and current account deficit in absolute terms, of about 15 to 20 billion dollars per annum, the inflows of foreign finance in embarrassingly racing in India to breach the mark of US$ 100 billion before long by way of foreign exchange reserves, is a telling piece of evidence of the success of the globalization policy package as a debt-collection and debt-market expansion policy for the corpulent financial markets of the rich countries. After all, one stated reason for going in for the present globalization path of development in India was the strong, supposedly national honour-based urge to avoid the shame and embarrassment of defaulting on the nation's external debt-servicing obligations. That one must borrow from the international markets on extremely difficult terms even for financing non-foreign exchange requiring activities and projects was apparently not considered a matter of national shame! Whether and how far the objectives of the creditor nations and their international organs like the World Bank, IMF, etc., to serve the interest of the international financial oligarchies by means of propagating and virtually imposing the SAP package are capable, at the same time, to satisfy the national urge and need for sustained and substantial broad-based growth along with a whole host of social and nationalistic objectives, can easily be imagined. The outcomes produced by these policies across the world do not seem to justify the presumed harmony of the interests and objective of these two sets of countries.

Let us not forget that the life of the present brand of globalization in operation since about the mid-1970s has been practically equally long compared to that of the earlier period's non-delinking- based mimetic, state-led growth approaches, (say from about the end of the Second World War to the first oil price hike by the OPEC countries). The latter gives some inherent advantage to the early industrializers. What is implied is that so long as the content, parameters and meaning of development remain externally derived or given, in the context of an unsavory legacy of the long dark period of continued, many-sided disempowerment of the Third World, its largest sections of people would not be able to participate and become co-sharers in the processes of modernization and industrialization. This is likely to be an inevitable feature of these processes unless conscious mobilization and even small micro-level beginnings are made to overcome the enfeeblement of the small and moribund communities, occupations and remote and deprived regions. The reason is not far to seek. The processes of globalization give rise to the possibility of convergence and divergence in varying proportions. Both are likely and are not mutually exclusive.

It depends on the actual course and content of development approach whether in a given situation convergence or divergence turns out to be stronger and asserts its supremacy basically by way of auto-centric development. The actual resolution of this conflict between the processes of convergence and divergence involves the entire political economy of development. What we have seen and is relevant for our present discussion is that the centre of the Centre, in close association with the centre of the Periphery, and by incorporating the intermediate strata by means of arousing their hopes and aspirations, has imposed on the world a market totalitarianism and presented it to the world as some kind of benign and inexorable necessity. Thus, what is taking place in the name and garb of globalization, is a mal-integration of the poorer societies on highly asymmetric and injurious terms and for fulfilling an agenda which is exogenous and non-responsive to the needs and aspirations of the people and nations who have been denied, deprived and disempowered by the processes of Social Darwinism unleashed on a global scale by the new social system which emerged in the wake of, among other factors, the scientific and technological revolutions of the last 500 years or so. Thus, what the really existing globalization the world is witnessing represents the very antithesis of development understood as real and effective collective self-empowerment of the people and, by the same token, works to deny justice to the poor and deprived. Collective self-empowerment, which is what development is all about, can become the agenda of the day only by doing away with the reigning globalization as the ideology, agenda and be-all of the MNEs and the states of their home nations which, of course, has to be supplemented in a big way by dethronement of the domestic turf allies and collaborators of the pernicious globalization which has so quickly

disillusioned so many all over the world. It is for the Third World social scientists to take up the gauntlet in order to get rid of the universal mal-development that has so unfortunately been imposed on humanity all over in the name of globalization.

References and Select Bibliography

1. Aghion Philippe & G. Williamson Jeffrey (Eds.) (1999). *Growth, Inequality, and Globalization: Theory, History and Policy,* Cambridge Univ. Press.
2. Amin, Samir (1977). *Capitalism in the Age of Globalisation: The Management of Contemporary Society,* London: Zed Books.
3. Bauman, Zygmunt (2000). *What is Globalisation?* Cambridge: Policy Press.
4. Bienfeld, Manfred (1993). *Structural Adjustment:* Debt Collection Device or Development Policy? Tokyo: Sophia University, Institute of Comparative Culture.
5. Brandt W. (1980). *North-South: A Programme for Survival,* Report of the Independent Commission on International Development Issues, London and Sydney: PAN Books.
6. Bryan, Lowell & Diana Farrell (1996). *Market Unbound: Unleashing Global Capitalism,* New York, Wiley.
7. Buelens, Frans (2000). *Globalisation and the Nation-State,* Northampton, MA: Edward Elgar Publishing.
8. Cable, V. (1999). *Globalisation and Global Governance,* London: The Royal Institute of International Affairs.
9. Carroll, William, Radhika Desai, & Warren Magnusson (1996). Globalisation, Social Justice and Social Movements: A Reader, Victoria, ON: University of Victoria.
10. Chalam, K.S. (1999). *Readings in Political Economy,* Hyderabad: Orient Longman.
11. Chomsky, Noam (1999). *Profit Over People: Neoliberalism and Global Order,* New York: Seven Stories Press.

12. DeMartino, George F. (1999), *Global Economy, Global Justice: Theoretical Objections and Policy Alternatives To Neoliberalism,* London: Routledge.
13. DeMartino, George F. (2001). *Democratizing the global Economy: The Battle Against the World Bank and the IMF,* Monroe, ME: Common Courage Press.
14. Falk, Richard A. (1999). *Predatory Globalisation: A Critique,* Cambridge: Polity Press.
15. Freemen, R.V. (Eds.) (2002). *Inequality Around the World,* New York, Palgrave.
16. Friedman, Thomas (2000). *The Lexus and the Olive Tree,* New York, Anchor Books.
17. Germain, Randall D. (2000). *Globalisation and Its Critics: Perspectives from Political Economy.* New York: St. Martin's Press.
18. Gilpin, Robert (2000). *The Challenge of Global Capitalism: The World Economy in the 21st Century,* Princeton, NJ: Princeton University Press.
19. Golding Peter & Harris, Phil (Eds) (1997). *Beyond Cultural Imperialism: Globalization, Communication and The New International Order,* London: Sage.
20. Gray, John (1998). *False Dawn: The Delusions of Global Capitalism,* New York: New Press.
21. Griffin Keith (Eds.) (1996). *Studies in Globalization and Economic Transitions,* London: Macmillan Press.
22. Hands-Heinrich, N. (2003). "Why is Europe's south poor: A chairs of International Peripheries." Review, 26 (1).
23. Hart, Jeffrey A. & Aseem Prakash (2000). *Coping with Globalisation,* London: Routledge.
24. Hoogvelt, Ankie (Eds.) (1997). *Globalisation and the Postcolonial World: The New Political Economy of Development,* London: Macmillan.
25. Iwasaki, T. et al (1992). *Development Strategies for the 21st century,* Tokyo: Institute f Developing Economies.
26. Kabra, Kamal Nayan (2002). "Globalisation and governance: Cloning the new millenium" in Reddy, N.D., Singh, S. & Arora, Dolly (Eds.) *Political Economy of WTO Regime: Some Aspects Of Globalisation And Governance,* New Delhi: Indian Political Economy Association and Rainbow Publishers.
27. Lechner, Frank J. & John Boli (Eds) (2000). *The Globalisation Reader,* Oxford: Blackwell.
28. Lindberg, Staffan & Sverrisson, Arni (Eds) (1997). *Social Movements in Development: The Challenge of Globalization and Democratization,* London: Macmillan.
29. Mark Lewis et al (1996). *The Growth of Nations: Culture, Competitiveness, and the Problem of Globalisation,* Bristol: Academic Press.
30. Martin, Hans-Peter, and Harald Schumann (1997). *The global trap: Globalisation and the assault on democracy and prosperity,* London: Zed Books.
31. Mask, Rupert (1997). *Contesting Hegemony: American and Far-Right Ideologies and of Globalization in Constituting International Political Economy*, (Eds.) Burch, K and Denemark, R.K. Boulder, London: Lynne Reinner Publishers.

32. Munck Ronaldo & O'Hearn, Denis (Eds.) (1999). *Critical Development Theory: Contributions to a New Paradigm,* London: Zed Books.
33. Nayyar, Deepak (Eds.) (2002). *Governing Globalisation: Issues and Institution,* New Delhi: Oxford University Press.
34. RIS (2003). *World Trade and Development Report, 2003: Cancun and Beyond,* New Delhi: Academic Foundation.
35. Rahnema, M. & Bawtree (Eds.) (1997). *The Post-Development Reader,* London: Zed Books.
36. Rodrik, Dani (1997). *Has Globalisation Gone Too Far?* Washington, DC: Institute for International Economics.
37. Rupert, Mark (2000). *Ideologies of Globalisation: Contending Visions of a New World Order,* London: Routledge.
38. Schuuman, F.J. (Eds.) (2001). *Globalisation and Development Studies: Challenges for the 21st Century,* New Delhi: Vistaar.
39. Soros, George. (1998). *The Crisis of Global Capitalism: Open Society Endangered,* New York: Public Affairs.
40. Steger, M.B. and Boulder (2002). *Globalisation,* London: Rowman & Littlefield Publication.
41. Strange, Susan (1997). *Mad Money: When Markets Outgrow Governments,* Ann Arbor: University of Michigan Press.
42. Tabb, William K. (2001). *The Amoral Elephant: Globalisation and the Struggle for Social Justice in the Twenty-first Century,* New York: Monthly Review Press.
43. Thimmons, J. (Eds.) (2000). *From Modernisation to Globalization Perspectives on Development And Social Change,* Malden: Blackwell.
44. Tomlinson, John (1999), *Globalisation and Culture,* Chicago: University of Chicago Press.
45. Tony S. (Eds.) (1996). *Globalisation and World Society,* Cambridge: Polity Press.
46. Wilber, L. K. & Johnson K.P. (Eds.) (1992), *The Political Economy & Development and Underdevelopment,* (5th edn), New York: McGraw Hill Inc.
47. World Bank (1998). *Global Economic Prospects and Developing Countries: Beyond Financial Crisis,* Washington: World Bank.
48. World Bank (2001). *Globalisation, Growth & Poverty: Building an Inclusive World Economy,* Washington, D.C.

The Good Boatman

Raj Mohan Gandhi

The fresh wave of globalization since the early 1990s has created a feeling of awe among the development researchers and practitioners, irrespective of the position they take on the type of economic development and one gets a feeling from the writings that something unprecedented is happening around the globe. However, globalization is not a totally new phenomenon although the nature of it in the 21st century might be somewhat different. Mahatma Gandhi, who made an overwhelming impact on the Indian freedom movement, had witnessed the British Society after the Industrial Revolution and had experienced the British rule in India and South Africa and had formulated his critique on it. He was also acutely aware of the impact of the British on the Indian intelligentsia and was not very happy about what lay in future for India, whether it would sway in this wave of westernization. The impact of the British on its colonies, according to him, was the impact of globalization that was taking place. Thus, about a hundred years ago, globalization had troubled the thinkers and political activists but in a somewhat different context. Swami Vivekananda also evoked a deep response in people of India and the world when he tried to re-interpret the notion of service of the God in the service of the poor and miserable people (Iyengar 2001). He was also thinking about the influence of western philosophy on the minds of the elite in India, which had almost in wholesale rejected the Indian intellectual tradition that had its base in religion. Over the centuries the Indian intellectual tradition had stagnated, rusted and had almost got reduced to a bundle of rituals immersed deeply in the degenerating caste system. Swami Vivekanand was perhaps worried about the cultural hegemony which the colonization threatened to bring. Thus, anxiety about globalization persisted even about a hundred years back and it has continued in one way or the other. Gandhi commented and critiqued more closely on the economic aspects and implications of adopting the western civilization as a model for development and in the process also warned against the possible cultural hegemony. In this paper, an attempt is made to excise Gandhi's thought and relate it with the present issues that are discussed in the context of globalization.

I wish to begin my reflections on Gandhian economic thought in the context of globalization and changing international economic scene with reference to *Hind Swaraj*, a book that Gandhi wrote and published in 1909, because Gandhi's thoughts on economics and subsequent development of Gandhian economic thought can be perhaps traded with *Hind Swaraj*, in which Gandhiji has mainly assessed the modernization of England and Europe and has anticipated the ill effects of it on the Indian society if the latter tried to follow the former blindly. After highlighting the point that emerges from *Hind Swaraj* with respect to economics, I plan to undertake a brief review covering comments on the status of contemporary society in India and outside. I will then look at the trends that are getting set in the new economic environment under the broad rubric of globalization and finally analyze the relevance or otherwise of the underlying principles in Gandhian economic thought.

Rajmohan Gandhi (1995) in his chapter titled "Hind Swaraj" notes the following in the "I for one am unable to accept the sweeping statement: The tendency of the Indian Civilization is to elevate the moral being that of the Western civilization is to propagate immorality. The latter is godless, the former is based on a belief in God' (Ch. 13). The torch held by *Hind Swaraj's* author does not throw an even light on the terrain under examination. Some portions remain in darkness while the shape of others is distorted or exaggerated. Yet no study of the historic encounter between the Indian and the western civilizations can ignore Hind Swaraj, neither can any study of the working of Gandhi's mind" (p. 139).

Gandhi wrote *Hind Swaraj* in 1909. On December 22, 1916, he responded to Kapildeva Malaviya's invitation to speak to the members of the Muir Central College Economic Society, Allahabad, and he delivered the talk titled, "Does Economic Progress Clash With Real Progress?" That is perhaps the nearest he came to comment upon Economics as a discipline and what he had to say about it. And while doing so, he was acutely aware of his limitations on the subject of Economics, yet he thought that the people belonging to that discipline should perhaps think on what he had to other, as his understanding of the subject should be also doing.

"Frankly and truly, I know little of economics, as you naturally understand it. Only the other day, sitting for an evening meal, a civilian friend deluged me with a series of questions on my crankisms. As he proceeded in his cross-examinations, I being a willing victim, he found no difficulty in discovering my gross ignorance of the matters. I appeared to him to be handling with cocksureness worthy only of a man who knows not that he knows not. To his horror and even indignation, I suppose he found that I had not even read books on economics by such well-known authorities as Mill, Marshall, Adam Smith, and a host of other such authors. In despair, he ended by advising me to read those books before experimenting in matters economic at the expense of the public. He little knew that I was a sinner past redemption. My experiments continue at the expense of trusting friends. But there come to us moment in life when about some things we need no proof from without. A little voice within us tells us, "You are on the right track, turn neither to your left nor right, but keep to the straight narrow way." (*Collected Works*, GoI, 2000, p. 273).

The tone he had set in Hind Swaraj continued in his 1916 lecture. He hardly changed later on in this matter, although he himself has said that he never had any final view on anything. His experiments and experiences gave him new insights. He has categorically mentioned that to know his position on any particular matter, one should always refer to his recent writings or utterances. On his thoughts on civilization and economic order that he had expressed in the *Hind Swaraj*, he declined to change even in 1939. He wrote a message for the February 1938 edition in September 1938 and which was published in an English monthly *Iron Path*', that if he were to write the *Hind Swaraj* again, he would only change the language here and there but would change very little of the original position that he had taken in 1909. The central thesis which he maintained was about the moral progress vis-a-vis material progress and as is clear from his 1916 lecture, the former was the real progress.

To the group of economists and other professors and scholars who had gathered that evening in the college in Allahabad, what did Gandhi have to offer? Let me first start with his statement about the inner voice that according to him guides the action in the 'right' direction during some critical moments in life. Obviously, this peculiar position would not be acceptable to many of his scholar friends. Gandhiji, by invoking the strength of the inner voice, admitted that he was taking the position without going through the intellectual exercise of the body of knowledge which existed at that point in time. But he said that he was convinced about the position he took. '…by economic progress, I take it, it means material progress without limit and by real progress we mean moral progress, which again is the same thing as progress of the permanent element in us' (*Collected Works* Vol. 15, p. 274). He has then commented upon material progress without limits.

According to him, the societies which had prospered materially, experienced a moral fall later. Rome, for instance, suffered a moral downfall after it achieved material affluence. The Yadavas ruined themselves morally when they were rolling in wealth. Gandhiji believed that an ordinary measure of morality is possessed by most of us, including the very rich, but material gain by did not ensure moral richness. Sharing his long-standing observation of society and the rich people, he said, 'I observed almost invariably that the greater the possession of riches, the greater was their moral turpitude. Our rich men, to say the least, did not advance the moral struggle of passive resistance, as did the poor. The rich man's sense of self-respect was not so much injured as that of the poor. If I were not afraid of treading on dangerous ground, I would even come nearer home and show you that possession of riches has been a hindrance to real growth'. Gandhiji then says that Jesus Christ was the greatest economist of his time. Quoting the dialogue between

Christ, a citizen and other disciples described by St. Mark, Gandhiji emphasizes in the lecture, the virtue of sharing wealth in the service of the poor and have-nots. The point that he brings out is against amassing wealth. Later he formulated *aparigrha* (non-accumulation) as one of the important presence of the English professors and scholars in the gathering. He appeared aware of this because he makes the point, ' I have not taken the trouble of copying similar passages from the other non -Hindu scriptures and I will not insult you by quoting in support of the law started by Jesus, passages from writings and sayings of our sages, passages stronger even if possible than the Biblical extracts have drawn your attention to ...Jesus, Mohamad, Buddha, Nanak, Kabir, Chaitanya, Shankara, Dayanand, Ramkrishna were men who exercised an immense influence over and moulded the character of men .... And they were all men who deliberately embraced poverty as their lot'. (*Collected Works*, 2000, Vol. 15, p. 276).

Gandhiji then talks about the craze for materialistic progress and argues that pursuing materialistic goals is a fall from idea. He says, "that you cannot serve [both] God and mammon is an economic truth of the highest value" (*Collected Works*, 2000, p. 277). He recommends building a truly spiritual nation (not by boasting about the glorious past) sought the kingdom of God that would be real economics.

It can be easily seen that his reservation was about the pursuit of limitless material prosperity in society. Gandhiji in *Hind Swaraj* explains the implications of fall in the moral standards in society following material prosperity. England was the most prosperous nation in the world when the *Hind Swaraj* was penned. The First World War was still five years away. America was already emerging as a land of great wealth. In his December 1916 lecture, he talks against America emerging as the role model for material progress. Gandhiji's reflections on modern civilization was largely based on the condition in England. In fact, in Chapter 5 entitled "Condition of England", Gandhiji criticizes parliament as an institution governing society. The central concern of Gandhiji was that the politicians in British Parliament were only interested in capturing and retaining political power and were by and large not worried about the welfare of the people. He also criticized the media for not being serious about assessing people and events and guiding them abjectively in assessing their leaders. Towards the end of the chapter, he ascribes the poor state of affairs in England to modern civilization when he says, 'it is not due to any peculiar fault of the English people, but the condition is due to modern civilization. It is civilization only in name. Under it the nations of Europe are becoming degraded and ruined day by day' (Parel 1997, p. 33).

The next chapter in *Hind Swaraj* is on civilization. Gandhi in this chapter says that people thought that living in better built houses, wearing fashionable clothes and wearing shoes was all part of civilized society, and now instead of spears, people carry revolvers containing five or more chambers. Ploughing land with steam engines and making wealth is considered a sign of civilization. Flying from one place to another is considered the height of civilization. He visualizes the future in the following manner: 'As men progress, they shall be able to travel in airships and reach any part of the world in a few hours. Men will not need the use of their hands and feet. They will press a button [and]have their clothing by their side. Another button and they will have their newspaper [beside them]. A third button and a motorcar will be waiting for them. They will have a variety of delicately dished up food.... Formerly, when people wanted to fight one another, they measured between them their strength; now it is possible to take away thousands of lives by one man working behind a gun from a hill. This is civilization." (Parel 1977, p. 36).

What Gandhiji saw in England during his stay made a deep impression reflected in the following way in the *Hind Swaraj*. 'Civilization seeks to increase bodily comforts, and it fails miserably even in doing so. The Civilization is irreligion, and it has taken such a hold on the people in England that those who are in it appear to be half mad. They lack real physical strength or courage. They keep up their energy by intoxication. They can hardly be happy in solitude. Women, who should be queens of their household, wander in the streets, or they slave away in factories. For the sake of a pittance, half a million women in England alone are labouring under trying circumstances in factories or similar institutions' (Parel 1997, p. 37).

Bodily comfort and a rush to acquire it is what Gandhiji has criticized most. In his December 1916 lecture, he introduced the concept of voluntary poverty. The saints and reformers he mentions were during their times living examples of voluntary poverty in order to achieve high moral standards. It is clear from *Hind Swaraj* and the lecture that material prosperity did not ensure high moral standards, instead, the dash for material prosperity brought the moral standards down and led to decay of the society. By these thoughts Gandhiji laid the philosophical foundation of the economic order for the society. According to him, limitless material progress could not be the goal of economic development in a society. Material progress is important only for very limited purposes of bringing people above from abject poverty and destitution which lowered or destroyed human dignity. The production and distribution system that Gandhi conceived and tried later in India along with the freedom struggle, calling it 'Swadeshi' movement, was founded on the basic tenet of ultimate moral progress with dignified and healthy physical survival.

Are Societies Decaying?

Since Gandhiji did not change his views on the desirable economic systems and his assessment of Western society, it may be useful to take a look at the world after 1948, the year in which Gandhiji was assassinated. Obviously, here I do not intend to undertake a comprehensive review of how the societies have developed in all parts of the world because it would imply country- or region-wise review of economic, social and cultural development. It is also obvious that there would be various views favouring or opposing development. A very limited exercise is undertaken here of reviewing some works by scholars who have been interested in Gandhian economic thought and development of society based on it.

Did Gandhi change his thinking on economic issues and his view on 'modern' civilization? As I have stated earlier, he did not do so at least until 1938 when a new edition of *Hind Swaraj* was published. What has been the assessment of some others about the changing world? Jai Prakash Narayan writing a Foreword in J.D. Sethi's book says, 'I do not deny that there has been considerable progress in the past thirty years in the economic field and that remains our very valuable asset. But along with that our problems and liabilities have become far more serious and menacing. The polity and its institutions have been seriously eroded. Some institutions have been destroyed just to satisfy the lust for power of one or a few individuals.... The moral fiber of our society has been shred to pieces'. (Sethi 1978, p. viii).

Sethi himself while writing a foreword for the book seven years later in 1985, comments on the Indian society (Diwan & Lutz, 1985). He says that the new economic problem was that of insatiability created by contrived wants, artificially boosted consumption through credit, and installment planning and structural inflation. Continuous expansion of production produced new environmental problems, which have created threats of new kinds. Real scarcity has been contrived scarcity, and as Harry Johnson has remarked, 'the successful definition of economy depends on reiterating the contrivance' (as quoted by Sethi in Diwan & Lutz 1985, p. XV). Gandhi would have termed this as falling morals due to greed.

Diwan & Lutz have the following to say on the American society which has undoubtedly attained immense economic prosperity compared to all other nations in the world. The context is of discussion on benevolence and malevolence in welfare economics. They note, 'in the rich countries, the quality of life is deteriorating even if the standard of living has phenomenally improved. The value of family life and other social values are breaking down. A substantial number of children have never lived with both their parents. The single-parent household is in the process of becoming the majority of the households in United States. Kidnapping and various forms of child abuse are now a national phenomenon. The adult life is marred by anxiety and job stress. Work for a large majority of workers is both stressful and meaningless. There is a growing scarcity of joy or pride in the work done. Old age is full of loneliness. Life has no doubt been prolonged but the lifestyle in many places has become more like a nightmare.... Crime has become so commonplace that police often cannot even care about burglaries, even rape, being busy as they are with murders and other serious injuries' (Diwan & Lutz, 1985 pp. 3-4).

I have mentioned earlier that Gandhiji had noted very early that America was emerging as the center of great material progress and it turned out to be correct. The role model for today for the developing nations is the USA, where a majority of aspiring youth from all over the world wants to settle down. Diwan continues to comment on the state of American society even in 1991. He says, 'even on material count, U.S. is facing set back at least in the 1980s. One may argue that the situation might improve, but one will have to admit that it would be fluctuating and there is no scope for consistent improvement of material progress. Continued and sustained growth in GDP and PCI are thus a false dream.' 'Expressed in 1977 prices, the average hourly earnings in 1970 was

$ 4.89 in 1980 and $ 4.84 in 1988. The statistics becomes more meaningful when looked at in terms of weekly earnings. In 1977, the weekly earnings fell down from $ 187 in 1970 to $ 168 in 1988...' (Diwan 1991). Youth were so hopeless that they did not even register themselves in the Employment Exchange and hence they are not counted. Many of these unemployed youth obviously joined the crime world and syndicates. The crime scene in U.S. was not encouraging in the 1980s. Diwan has observed that murder, rape, robbery and aggravated assault had risen exponentially. The number of violent crimes increased from 1,208,000 in 1979 to 1,566,000 in 1988. The public expenditure on criminal justice system increased from $ 10,517 million in 1971 to $ 45,607 million in 1985, i.e. by a whopping 334 per cent! The numbers of prisoners have also swelled. Today U.S. has the dubious distinction of having the highest number of incarcerated individuals in prison!

Medical services were expensive in the US, and in 1985-86, some 34 million people, or about 15 per cent of the U.S. population, were not covered by any private or public health insurance. Diwan thus notes that there was an emergence of an underclass in the U.S. and that the economic maintenance of the family required more than one earner. Women joining the work force in large numbers has had serious impact on family make-up and structure. He notes that the social life in the U.S has been deteriorating. The average size of households declined from 3.33 in 1960 to 2.76 in 1980 and to 2.62 in 1988. The percentage of families having their own biological children had fallen to 52 per cent in 1980. Diwan then goes on to look at an American from birth to death and describes the process of human being goes through. One can only conclude such a description by saying that 'among a plethora of plenty people perish' (Michael Lipton, 1980).

Thus, about a century after Gandhi had commented on the problems in pursuing material progress and the type of the society that England was, America, which was the next to emerge and indeed has emerged as the richest and most materially advanced country in the world, does not seem to offer any better role model. As one reflects on the American lifestyle, one cannot help commenting that if this were the life a person sought in one of the richest countries in the world, it is by no standards a satisfactory lifestyle. More recently, the statistics published by the US Census Bureau recorded a poverty level of 11.3 per cent in 2000, which was lower than 11.8 per cent in 1999. Incidentally, 11.3 per cent, the figure recorded in 1973 has been the lowest ever recorded figure. This only means that between 1973 and 1999, poverty levels were always above the lowest mark recorded in 1973. In 2001-03, 38.2 per cent of all children below 19 years of age were 200 per cent below poverty level income and about 20 per cent of them were not covered under health insurance. Unemployment rates have been a little above 5 per cent between 1995 and 2004. According to the Bureau of Labour Statistics, the unemployment rate ranged between 5.4 and 5.7 per cent during January-December 1995, and in 2004 to the range was same. This is consistent with the persistent poverty ratio too. Unemployment rates have been mostly in this range. It touched a record low of 3.8 per cent in 1999 and had been less than 5 per cent in most months during 1997 and 2001. However, it had risen to 6.3 in a month during 2003.

Crime rates have come down between 1993 and 2003 from more than 4 million to less than 2 million, according to the US Census Bureau charts. But there has been a steady rise in number of people convicted for felony between 1988 and 2002 from about 750,000 to more than 1000,000. Similarly, among the correctional institutions, percentage under probation in 1980 was 61 and it came down to 58 in 2003. This means that more numbers were either in prison or on parole. The Bureau of Justice's statistics recorded that the number of adults in correctional institutions has been increasing. It rose from 1.8 million in 1980 to 6.4 million in 2003. Thus, from the material progress and moral progress points of view, American society fails to provide a role model. To this extent, Gandhiji's critique on the western civilization and progress would be significantly relevant even today although the moral decay of the society might not have been as substantial as Gandhiji had tried to visualize. However, since his criticism of the western civilization and the unsuitability of it in the Indian case, some more aspects have cropped up that raise questions on the desirability of the adoption and continuation of the concepts and practices of the western civilization.

Gandhiji's views both on the world order as well as the economic development of society, did not find place in the main development agenda of most societies in the world, including India. What Gandhiji had termed as "western civilization" was largely followed by developing nations, though some countries adopted central planning as the means to achieve the goals of modern civilization. Changing the social fabric and moral standards of society has been relegated to the background. One of the Indian scholars speaking about Gandhi's economic thoughts and its relevance in 1985 at an Economic Conference argued that the new phase of industrial revolution had come to respecting trained human individuals more and man has returned to center stage away from the machine and hence there was some congruence in what Gandhi was saying and what the world tended to follow (Siddharthan 1985). The human-centric information revolution also did not make any headway towards welfare of all human beings; instead it gave rise to another problem that had hitherto not appeared so distinctly, although a group of scientists had started worrying about it. A remarkable document titled "The Limits to Growth was by a small team at the Massachusetts Institute of Technology in US, which studied the fundamental limits to growth in the global population, agriculture, resource use, industry and pollution. Economic growth under the modern civilization had created immense pressure on the natural resource base such as land, forest, water and air. Overexploitation and pollution are two main menaces in the context of the overuse of both renewable and non-renewable natural resources. A new movement, namely, environment movement, has emerged and it is fairly powerful. Morality and values have been brought to discussion via the irreversible damages being caused to nature. The conventional development models have supposedly led to disaster and destruction. 'Sustainable Development' is the concern of the groups spearheading the environmental movement.[ii] There is a lot of literature reflecting the views and analysis based on environmental concerns. In this paper, its review is not attempted. But it is relevant to note that the scholars, activists and practitioners basing their work on Gandhian thought have clearly sided with the environmental movement in the world in general and in the country in particular. There have been some serious arguments relating the present crisis and it is argued that had the societies followed the Gandhian path, the possibility of achieving sustainable development might have been higher.

Globalization: The New Trend

After about 80 years of Gandhiji's comment on the dangers of adopting the means and methods of western civilization, the pressure is once again high to globalize. By globalization is meant adoption of the process of development that has been practiced and favoured by the countries in Europe and the USA or what is broadly categorized under the 'North'. There is a tremendous pressure building up in most countries, developed or otherwise, to allow free trade. Free movement of goods and services across the border is supposedly beneficial to one and all. It is argued that because of the development of science and technology distances have died and there is everything to gain if world economy is closely interlinked. With close trade relations there is a higher possibility of world peace. Many perceive globalization as a primarily economic phenomenon, involving the increasing interaction or integration, of national economic systems through the growth in international trade, investment and capital flows. However, one can also consider rapid increases in cross-border social, cultural and technological exchanges as part of the phenomenon of globalization.

The English sociologist Anthony Giddens defines globalization as a decoupling of space and time, emphasizing that with instantaneous communications, knowledge and culture can be shared around the world simultaneously (Gullen Mauro F., 2001). A Dutch scholar Ruud Lubbers defines it as a process in which geographic distance becomes a factor of diminishing importance in the establishment and maintenance of cross border economic, political and socio-cultural relations. Leftist critics of globalization define the world quite differently, presenting it as a worldwide drive toward a globalized economic system dominated by super national corporate trade and banking institutions that are not accountable to democratic process or national governments. Yet another view suggests that globalization is an undeniably capitalist process. It has taken off as a concept after the collapse of the Soviet Union and of socialism as a viable alternate form of economic organization.

When did globalization actually start there is no agreed starting point but considering the following helps understanding globalization. The first great expansion of European capitalism took place in the 16th century, following the first circumnavigation of the earth from 1519 to 1521, although this is the explanation of Western history. India carried out international trade even before the Christian era began, that too was a kind of globalization. There was big expansion in world trade and investment in the last 19th century. The First World War and the bout of anti-free trade protectionism that led to the Great Depression in 1930 brought this to a halt. Some see this period as an interruption to the process of globalization which commenced in the late 19th century.

Seeing from another perspective, a sense was generated that the world was united by the establishment of the International Date Line and world time zones, together with the near global adoption of the Gregorian Calendar between 1875 and 1925. During that period, international standards were also agreed for telegraphy and signaling. The end of the Second World War brought another great expansion of capitalism with the development of multinational companies interested in producing and selling in the domestic markets of nations around the world. The emancipation of the colonies created a new world order. Air travel and the development of international communications enhance the progress of international business. The fall of the Berlin Wall and the collapse of the Soviet Union ended the Cold War between the forces of capitalism and socialism with capitalism triumphant. The development of the Internet made possible the organization of business on a global scale with greater facility than ever before.

The chief concerns with respect to globalization that are being addressed are five, as listed by Wharton School sociologist Guillen (2000).

- It is really happening?
- Does it produce convergence?
- Does it undermine the authority of the nation state?
- Is globality different from modernity?
- Is a global culture in the making?

The believers and especially practitioners of Gandhian thought and philosophy by and large have taken an anti-globalization stand. In their understanding, globalization is harmful and anti- Gandhian. Globalization means onslaught of foreign capital and technology destroying the inland systems of production, exploitation of workers in the poor countries and most importantly, cultural invasion and market expansion. Most of them think that it is really happening and will ultimately undermine the autonomy and authority of nation states. Multinational National Companies (MNCs) are specially targeted for attack and it is its postulated that the MNCs will ultimately undermine the authority of the nation state. The debate in literature on the cultural invasion and market expansion has brought that the main player that is also definitely gaining in America. In fact, the perceived that is thread on Americanization'.

When cross- border trade in goods and services take place, some cultural integration is also bound to happen. A report by the UN Educational, Scientific and Cultural Organization (UNESCO), showed that the world trade in goods with cultural content almost tripled between 1980 and 1991 from 67 billion dollars to 200 billion dollars. These figures would have further scaled new heights. At the core of the entertainment industry -- film, music and television --there is a growing dominance of US products. World Trade Organization rules do not allow countries to block imports on.

It is argued that one of the consequences of globalization will be the end of cultural diversity and the triumph of a unipolar culture serving the needs of transnational corporations. Hence, the world drinks Coco-cola, watches American movies and eats American fast-food. English is the language of globalization; by 2050, it is surmised, that half the world will be more or less proficient in English. What are the implications for languages as repositories of culture and identity? American culture is seen to be dominated by monetary relationships and commercial values replacing traditional social relationship and family values.

Gandhiji in his *Hind Swaraj* and subsequent writings and utterances, was mainly concerned with the last two questions relating to modernity and global culture. His position on economic philosophy was more fundamental, relating it with morals and ethics for earning and spending. Similarly, he did define in his own way a modern civilization for Indians and India that had to be different from the then England and British. In the next section, therefore, I revisit the basic tents in Gandhian economics and then comment how globalization may be viewed in the Gandhian frame.

Gandhi's Economic Thought and Globalization

Gandhiji was keenly aware of the strong disagreement on his position on economics. Following his Lecture on December 22, 1916, the leader carried the story on December 25 and reported what Professor Stanley Jevons had commented[iii] on the previous evening after Gandhiji's lecture was over. He had said that though it was necessary for economists to exist, it was not their business to lay down what the end should be. That was the business of philosophers. Most likely, Professor Jevons might not have read the *Hind Swaraj* because Gandhiji has been so unequivocal on the issue of means and ends. Rajmohan Gandhi (1995) quotes Gandhiji on means and ends with respect to violence, which again is a value that was very central to the economic system propagated by him.

Rajmohan Gandhi says that Gandhiji's case on means and ends and against violence was compelling. 'If I want to cross the ocean, I can do so only by means of a vessel; if I were to use a cart for the purpose, both the cart and I would find the bottom.... The means may be linked to a seed, the end to a tree as there is the same inviolable connection between the means and the end as there is between the seed and the tree' (Rajmohan Gandhi, op. cit., p. 140).

Moral value was extremely important for Gandhiji. Economics without ethics and ethical consideration was not warranted. Dasgupta (1996) in his comprehensive analysis on Gandhi's economic thought has dealt with the subject thoroughly. According to him, Gandhi's approach to economic issues was explicitly based on ethical considerations. "Gandhi insisted that the relationship between economics and ethics works both ways. While economic concepts were laden with ethical implication, ethics too must descend from the clouds and become 'good economics'. Ethics, Gandhi is saying, is not simply an exercise for philosophers, a convenient handle for sharpening their wits on the logic of extreme. It must be relevant to the ordinary business of life where one's options are limited by resource constraints. Ethics by its nature is an enterprise for the worldly, a guide to the perplexed, and its answers, to be credible, need to be economically viable. "No person in the world has found to maintain something which is a source of constant economic loss" (Dasgupta, 1996, p.7).

The foregoing also clears Gandhiji from the possible branding of him as a deontologist. It is convincingly argued, and one must accept this, that Gandhiji was quintessentially a consequentialist. For him the individual was the unit. That is where the '*antyodaya*' has been born from John Ruskins' *Unto This Last.* He was an individualist and not a collectivist. Gandhiji argues that 'if the individual ceases to count, what is left of society? Social choice which was dictatorial or imposed could not properly be regarded as choice at all and Satyagraha in the form of non-violent non-cooperation always remained a valid option (Dasgupta, 1996).

Complicating it or making deliberate attempts to make the processes complex of society's economic functions, mainly the economic activities, and looking for smooth devices for solving the complexities that arise in economic transactions, needs to be distinguished. The use of science and technology for the latter is also not only useful but desirable too even within the framework of simple living and high thinking. At the time of writing the *Hind Swaraj*, Gandhiji had seen the efforts all over the world and especially England, which was the imperial lord of the world then, of complicating economic activities so that the one who set in complications reaped the maximum benefit by way of profit for the firm and industry and income and employment for the population. The criticism by the advocates of simple and uncomplicated societies for human survival, who also drew their basic strength from the emphasis on spiritual growth and development of human civilization rather than the materialistic growth and development, has been that the modernization of society with the beginning of industrialization has largely implied complicating economic transactions. The main reason for this is the acceptance of the premise that human wants are insatiable. And this has been accepted as such without any serious scrutiny with morals and ethics in the society. Sethi draws attention to this aspect in a very interesting Foreword that he wrote to the volume *Essays in Gandhian Economics* edited by Diwan and Lutz in 1985. He quotes Lionel Robbin's celebrated definition: "Economics is the science which studies human behaviour as a relationship between ends and scarce means which have alternative uses" (Diwan & Lutz 1985) and says that all that economics has been doing is the opposite of what Robbins said the discipline was to do!

From the foregoing analysis it should be clear that Gandhiji's thoughts on economics cannot be brought into the framework of the economics discipline as it has emerged. However, it is possible to explain the implications of Gandhiji's thoughts on economics on some of the microeconomics and macroeconomic tenets. The relevant questions in the present context are: (i) Would Gandhiji have been against international trade and thus globalization? (ii) Would Gandhiji have been against science and technology for removing poverty and unemployment? These two are the main questions because it is being argued by the mainstream economists that world poverty and unemployment can be removed with the application of modern science and technology in production and consumption of goods and services, and that the prime mover of sustained economic growth for any economy is free international trade.

There is no straight answer to these two central questions in Gandhiji's scheme of economic thought, and if we wish to understand Gandhi's basic premise of economics, we will have to start with the treatment of wants. Why did Gandhi suggest control of wants? He did so because he understood that human wants, given the freedom of choice, is insatiable. The societal approach to accept the insatiability of human demands and then use science and technology for want satisfaction, was not a sustainable approach according to him. Let us first examine the implication for individual behaviour in the microeconomics framework. Francis Edgeworth, the Anglo-Irish philosopher, said more than a century ago that the first principle of economics was that every agent was actuated only by self-interest (Diwan & Lutz, 1985). From there arises the maximization behaviour. It is from here that the 'economic man' was born.

This 'economic man' is unacceptable to Gandhiji. It is here that he parts company with standard economics. According to Dasgupta (1996), it is Gandhiji's conviction that one's behaviour as an economic agent cannot be isolated from one's behaviour as an autonomous moral agent. In this context, Gandhiji brings in self-restraint. Then he talks about limiting wants. In his scheme, wants cannot be unlimited and hence they would have to be controlled. The 'haves', should not be aspiring for more and more and more. Elaborating on this, M.N. Raval in a short article entitled "Contentment and Containment of Wants - A Suggested Interpretation", introduces the "Gandhi Effect," which has its basis in 'asceticism' and 'paternalism', in economics, consumption pattern among different income groups in society has been discussed and it has been argued that different income groups will have different consumption patterns. Veblen, the American economist and sociologist, had pointed out in this context that there is a tendency of emulation in consumption. He brought out that there is and would be 'vulgar display of wealth' by the handful of rich in society. This tendency was an important constraint on free choice. Duesenbury, the American economist, carried forward this analysis further and studied and analyzed cross-sectional variations in consumption expenditure of different income groups and termed this phenomenon "demonstration effect". Since the idea originated in Veblen's analysis it may also be termed as the "Veblen effect".

The economic man and the economic society are so defined that one always feels poor no matter how rich one is. The core of this contradiction lies in the consumption theory and not in the production theory. Let us remember what Marshall, the creator of the Consumption theory, had to say, "Although it is man's wants in the earliest stages of his development that give rise to his activities, yet afterwards each new step is to be regarded as the development of activities giving rise to new wants rather than of new wants giving rise to new activities" (Diwan &Lutz 1985). Despite this clear understanding that Marshall displayed with respect to contrived demand dominating the consumer behaviour, economists continued to accept 'consumer sovereignty'.

Gandhiji suggested a consumption pattern and behaviour for the affording classes that was to be moderated by ascetic and paternalistic values. Raval has termed this as the 'Gandhi Effect'. The individual preference function must be impacted by this. In positive economics, there is no scope to introduce this constraint and then maximize utility. Income is the only constraint that is accepted. Gandhiji had categorical suggestions for preferences. In a particular context (in his case, the freedom struggle), the individual preference for '*Swadeshi*'- home made-- was extremely important. Any economics that cannot incorporate this aspect was no good economics for him during the times he led the *ahimsak satyagaraha* against the British. "It is the normative concept of preference, which I shall call 'ethical preference', that lies at the heart of the Gandhian approach to economic theory" (Dasgupta 1996, p. 13). The issue is whether the Gandhian concept of ascetics and paternalism in consumer behavior can be incorporated in the modeling. Professor Kenneth Boulding (as referred by Raval 1971) has opined that it was possible. He says, "Man required both neurotic and economic elements in his institutions, in his learning process and in his decision making. ...The familiar tools (in economic theory) like the Indifference Map and the Edgeworth Box can easily be explained to include benevolence or malevolence. The assumption in the Demand theory that 'tastes are given' is a great illusion and would literally be true for 'birds' whose tastes are largely determined by their genetic structure and can therefore be treated as a constant. In human society, the genetic component is very small, and the largest part of human preference is "learned by means of mutation-selection process" (Raval 1971, p. 118). In Pareto's scheme of things too, welfare proposition does not admit any malevolence. Societal refers to a pure state of benevolence. If it is so, then Gandhiji is in. Welfare economics discusses two externalities, negative and positive, in consumption. The Veblen Effect may be treated as a case of negative externality, and in a similar vein, Gandhi Effect may be treated as a positive externality. The point is to internalize it.

Let me illustrate a case of contrived demand and how it is created in society in a most benign but sure way. You may be seeing that an advertisement in television appears repeatedly. It will definitely be one of the fast-moving consumer items and the firm producing it taking up an 'aggressive marketing strategy'. It could be, say, be a toothpaste advertisement. It conveys a message that eating chocolates and ice-cream at any time and in any quantity is fine because mothers should leave the worry of tooth decay to the toothpaste producer who guarantees that their toothpaste will help in fighting germs 24 hours and arrest tooth decay. The advertisement thus simultaneously promotes chocolates, ice-cream and in short, uncontrolled eating (read consumption) and promotes its own item of sale, that is, toothpaste, which according to them uses the latest scientific technology for fighting tooth decay. Such unbridled consumption clearly implies use of resources (that the neo-classical theory would promise us to believe has been optimally allocated!) that are indeed scarce. Modern parents who believe in the merits of science and technology in general human welfare are happy that unlike their parents they do not have to restrict their children from consuming more chocolates and ice-creams because the new toothpaste with will provide the necessary protection. Maybe they too could pop into their mouths a chocolate or two without any worry. The rise in demand for chocolates, ice-cream and toothpaste in response to the advertisement is a case of contrived demand. Science and dentists tell us that there is no need for any toothpaste to keep gums and teeth healthy.

Believing and justifying the toothpaste type of approach would lead to unsustainable use of our natural resource base. Interestingly, the development of ecological and environmental concerns and theorizing around that in economics, has already found legitimate space in global policy on environment. Efforts in valuation of ecological and environmental services using novel methods of sound and not so sound estimation methods are one, and the game still remains as to how we can get the Hotel rent rationalized and increase the probability for the application of the Hartwick rule. Ciracy Wantrup who talked about the looming ecological crisis and suggested conservation of the flagship species in nature, has been in a way relegated to the background (For a detailed discussion see Hanely et al., 1997). Mainstream economics is still highly reluctant to enter into a 'lifestyle' debate. Clearly, the 'lifestyle' is given as we saw in Boulding's statement that "tastes are given".

If taste is not given and can be influenced by generating Veblenian demonstration effect on the consumer, then Gandhian Effect too should find a place and the individual demand curve need not be downward sloping for all consumers. By influencing groups with more income (more than what is necessary to meet the basics of living), we may construct a demand curve for them that becomes income inelastic after a certain point (for theoretical discussions refer Brahmananda 1971). This would imply that after certain levels of consumption have been reached, additional income does not give rise to any new demand, including leisure. Control on demand would free certain resources that can be used to produce the requirements of those who will continue to have a downward sloping demand curve. It will also help in controlling the use of resources some of which may be overexploited. From this concept was born the refined concept of 'trusteeship'. I do not intend to pursue the trusteeship issues in this article.

Thus, the wants control theory of Gandhiji simultaneously solves the problem of consumerism and unsustainable resource use. The ecological and environmental economics disciplines try to grapple with the equilibrium analysis by internalizing the ecological and environmental externalities, but Gandhian economics by regulating individuals' wants and demand function, has the potential to regulate and control some of the externalities.

On the macroeconomic front too, Gandhiji was clearly promoting decentralized production systems. Village level self-sufficiency was nothing but providing maximum opportunity for production at the local level. He preferred simple systems as against modern systems that were complicated. Lakdawala's assessment on this issue about Gandhijii may be seen in the following expression. "Gandhiji instinctively disliked the working of the money or banking mechanism. The institution of money was too complex in his opinion; transactions in kind were more easily understood and more human. The only types of banks he approved were in the nature of grain banks for safe local storage. Ordinary commercial banks associated with urbanization were a part of the mechanism of local exploitation" (Lakdawala 1971, pp. 47-48).

Just because Gandhiji had an apparent dislike for complicated or complex economic systems does not imply that he was completely ignorant about the macro systems. Poverty and unemployment were uppermost in his mind. He invited Prof. C.N. Vakil, who was then heading the Bombay School of Economics then, to suggest how a country like India could get rid of the problem of poverty. Vakil's articles in *Young India* in the late 1920s invited very good comments as well as criticism from various national and international quarters. In this context, Sethi argues that Marxism, which was a critical response to the misery in English society after the abolition of Poor Law in 1836, also ironically, rested itself on the classical political economy and provided defense for it. No wonder that values and even simple compassion were considered enemies of Marxism as they had been banished from classical theory. In the name of efficiency, productivity, good management and reasonable return on capital, the corporate sector, with its growing monopolistic and oligopolistic and transnational character, has become the centre not only of economic power but also of the draconian and violent political power. The power of the state economic sector, instead of countervailing the corporate sector, has now become its ally. The alliance is however, losing its legitimacy because it has failed to take on the major economic issues of unemployment, poverty, inflation, inequality, etc. besides, the rise of new problems such as pollution, ecological imbalance, exhaustion of resources and massive diversion of resources to nuclear armament, etc. Problems, which were kept separate, now demand a joint solution. However, the economic complexities and crisis have not yet produced a corresponding political consciousness for a new political order that can integrate facts, problems and values.

By rejecting the market and its value systems are we saying that State is God? No, because in this case, God failed miserably. It was perhaps bound and many had warned about it (Shenoy was the most vocal in the case of India). The Vakil-Bramananda Wage Goods model also finally led to the same Market-State ideal combination that appeared to fail ultimately (for details refer Desai 1998). Did Gandhi think differently? It is again important to remember that Gandhiji, although he invited Vakil to write, did not completely agree with the measures suggested by Vakil. He wanted to attach the poverty problem with retaining the dignity of the self and the dignity of labour. His emphasis on human dignity and labour branded him as someone opposed to machines and therefore science and technology. It became easy to call him an old-timer or belonging to the traditional school and dismiss him. Only on this, one might be wrong to interpret that Gandhi was all for promoting subsistence economy only. Since he knew that his thoughts on economic systems were traditional and dated, he did not pursue them later. Some have also argued that the fact that Gandhiji chose Nehru as the Prime Minister was an indication that he wanted to see the country industrialize according to Nehru's vision. This version is also not true. Gandhiji was neither averse to science and technology nor did he push for subsistence economy. Let us take up the case of machines first.

Siddharthan (1985) has recounted an encounter of one Mr. Ramachandran with Gandhiji on the issue of machine and modernization (printed in the November 13, 1924 issue of *Young India*). Gandhiji was bluntly asked whether he was against machinery. Gandhiji categorically said that he was not against machinery as such, but he was certainly against all machinery that exploited people. He was also opposed to the craze for machinery. He would have certainly frowned upon the gadgets and the gizmos that the top executives carry and flaunt with pride today. (And the financial newspapers run special glossy supplements on such executive choices!). Saving labour for throwing people on the streets without work is what Gandhiji never accepted. Man was always at the centre and he too abhorred drudgery. Not surprisingly his comment on the invention of the sewing machine by Singer Company was the following:" It is one of the useful things ever invented and there is a romance about the device itself. He (Singer) devised the sewing machine in order to save her (his wife) from unnecessary labour. He however saved not only her from labour but also the labour of everyone who could purchase a sewing machine" (Siddharthan 1985, p. 35). Interestingly, surplus can also arise by squeezing labour and as capitalism advances it is technology which is used to throw labour out and to increase profits. Gandhiji had said it in a different way that machines for greed were not good and he would oppose them, but machines for supporting labour was always welcome.

Siddharthan (1985) analyses the Gandhian thoughts about machine and industry under four areas: Labour displacement and the consequent unemployment, factor proportions and resource advantage, drudgery of work and problems relating to distribution. He argues that in the first stages of Industrial Revolution, which England and other countries in the west went through, Gandhiji's concerns and critique was perhaps relevant and right. He also compares it with the Marxian analysis and says that both at one level had similar apprehensions. Siddharthan then writes a postscript in which he says that the fourth industrial revolution (fourth stage) was the Information Revolution. In this type, Gandhiji-type reservations are ruled out. Machinery, that is computer hardware and software skills, would be the key to economic progress. He then laments about the lack of literacy and educational drives in the country. Indeed in 1985 with 1981 literacy statistics that he quotes, the levels were indeed low. He argues that with increased literacy and skill levels there would be increasing employment. He predicts that India may be short of supply as the demand was going to be huge; it is about 20 years ago that Siddharthan made this prediction. He is right and wrong both. India has responded to the fourth or information revolution in an overwhelming fashion and yet it still contends with the unemployment problem.

Gandhiji's concern about the type of economic development model was thus relevant then and relevant even now. In a labour surplus economy, technology and industry have to be one supporting production by the masses rather than mass production. Gandhiji did not anticipate a western type of industrialization even in the 1930s when the population was around 350 million. In the September 14, 1934 issue of *Harijan* he wrote, "We can never industrialize India, unless of course, we reduce our population from 350 million to 35 million or hit upon markets wider than our own and dependent on us" (as quoted in Siddharthan 1985). Thus, Gandhiji was clear that capturing markets in other countries was one possible goal and removing drudgery and using capital in a labour scarce economy was another. Interestingly, today with even 1000 plus population, people in India argument would alter only slightly. Only 40 per cent people in India have the purchasing power for most of the industrial and consumer goods that are produced and the mega Indian companies are raring to capture the global markets and that is how all the support to globalization. Poverty and unemployment persist albeit at much lower proportions than what they were during Gandhiji's time. Industrialization of the fourth generation, i.e., Information and Technology (IT) type also has had limited advantage in solving the problem of poverty and unemployment.

The issue of creating or searching for new markets in the world brings us to the present-day situation again. What did Gandhi think about international trade? Obviously, he never wrote anything exclusively on it like he did on some other concepts such as trusteeship, *aparigraha*, village industry and Khadi. However, A.M. Huq (1985) in an interesting article has made a good attempt to interpret Gandhian thought on international trade. It is of course obvious and important to understand the concept of Swadeshi in this context. However, there is also a danger that while understanding Swadeshi one concludes that Gandhiji rejected the comparative advantage thesis. Huq constructs an interesting thesis of positive doctrine of international trade from the Gandhian perspective. It accepts the logic of comparative advantage but rejects it as the sole basis for trade among nations. Put differently, Gandhiji was in favour of fair trade more than free trade. His concept of fairness had an ample measure of non-economic sanctions too.

Let us reiterate Gandhiji's concept of Swadeshi once again. To quote Gandhiji (as quoted by Huq), 'A votary of Swadeshi will carefully study his environment, and try to help his neighbour wherever possible, by giving preference to local manufactures, even if they are of an interior grade or dearer in price than things manufactured elsewhere.... It is sinful for me to eat American wheat and let my neighbour, the grain dealer, starve for want of customers. Similarly, it is sinful for me to wear the latest finery of Regent Street when I know that if had but worn the things woven by the neighbouring spinners and weavers that would have clothed me, and led and clothed them'. This clearly is a case for supporting production by masses. His emphasis on Khadi and village industry would become amply clear from this quote of his. If non-economic value of supporting the neighbour is accepted, then the concept of Swadeshi is clear. The subsequent dogmatization of village self-sufficiency by Gandhiji's followers, also known as Sarvodaya people, if any, has to be seen in this light. Gandhiji was realistic enough to admit that no village or for that matter country was also clear that he was not talking about demands. Need, according to Gandhiji, is not demand because the former is weighed in terms of ethical values and the principles of non-violence in its production.

Gandhiji was thus not against international trade per say. He would impose economic and non-economic sanctions in a big way and to this extent would not allow free trade. Second, he also knew that relying solely on the comparative advantage does not help the poor nations to prosper because the powerful nations push their greed and manage to manipulate. Failure of talks of agriculture in WTO is a case in point. If we combine this aspect with the difference between the need and the demand (read contrived demand), cultural hegemony is also inevitable and Gandhiji was strongly Swadeshi as far culture is concerned.

Thus, once we understand these basic tenets in Gandhiji's economic thoughts, it becomes clear that globalization appears at a fairly late stage. In these writings, that are scattered, he has written to the effect that he was not against selling genuine surplus in the local economies. He was not averse to technologies and knowledge that reduced human misery and drudgery. It did not matter whether it was local or foreign. But it is also very clear that he never was in agreement that economies should be growing with export as the engine. By promoting that was local and helped in the generation of a dignified livelihood, the cultural onslaught from would by itself get minimized. In his scheme, globalization would not enter as it is poised today to influence the developing economies.

Looking back, one is amazed at the acute understanding of each of the problems Mahatma Gandhi had. He dealt with some problems more intensively than others, but he never lost sight of any of them. He denounced the concept of the economic man because he refused to recognize the separation of economics from ethics. He denounced technological determinism because it enslaved man and sanctified only those technologies that conformed to value premises. Above all, he struggled against the mightiest imperial power in terms of a non-violent theory and order. As he went along with these tasks, he discovered his own science of economics, although he did not analyze it in a very vigorous manner. He was not interested in the scope of and method of economic science, as we economists "naturally understand it". Rather, he worked for a lifetime on articulating the principle of an alternative and "more real" human economy centering on the very theme outlined in his 1916 Lecture: the lack of correlation between material expansion and genuine progress, the need for an economics-cum-ethics that will enable moral growth and dignity for all, the fallacy of seeking happiness in individual acquisitive behaviour, and the need for encouraging people to seek a life of self-esteem and genuine meaning.

This is a very modest attempt to review the literature that has appeared on Gandhian economics as has been put together by some academics who have made serious attempts to define the Gandhian paradigms sharply and with some rigour that lacked in the hands of the Gandhians. In their hands, as J.D. Sethi puts it, Gandhian Economics still remains immature, and he defines the term "immature" here as reflecting the numerous ill-defined paradigms. However, it is believed that the Gandhian approach is superior because its concepts lie in their in-built dynamics and close relations with praxis, implying that once on a Gandhian path, not only the system put on the path of steady growth, its moral legitimacy also does not remain in doubt any longer.

References

1. Brahmananda P.R. 1971. "A Theoretical Note on the Economic Foundation of a Gandhi type society" in Raval M.N. et. al. (Eds), *Gandhiji's Economic Thought and its Relevance at Present,* South Gujrat University, Surat.
2. Dasgupta Ajit K. 1996. *Gandhi's Economic Thought,* Routledge, London.
3. Desai Meghnad, 1988. "Development Perspective: Was there an Alternative to Mahalanobis", in Ahluwalia Isher Judge, Little I.M.D. (Eds.). 1998. *India's Economic Reforms and Development Essays, Oxford* University Press, Delhi.
4. Diwan Romesh and Lutz Mark (editors) 1985. Essays in Gandhian Economics, Gandhi Peace Foundation, New Delhi.
5. Gandhi Rajmohan 1956. The Good Boatman: *A Portrait of Gandhi,* Penguin Books, New Delhi.
6. Government of India 2000. *Collected Works of Mahatma Gandhi,* Volume 15, 4th revised edn, Publications Division, Ministry of Information and Broadcasting, GoI, New Delhi.
7. Gullien Mauro F. 2001. "Is Globalisation Civilising, Destructive or Feeble? A Critique of Five Key Database in the Social Science Literature", in *Annual Review of Sociology,* Vol. 27, 2001 Wharton School and Department of Sociology, University of Pennsylvania, USA.
8. Hanley Nik, Shogren Jason F. & White Ben 1997. *Environmental Economics in Theory and Practice,* Macmillan, Delhi.
9. Hug A.M. 1985. "The Doctrine of Internal Trade: A Gandhian Perspective". in Diwan Romesh and Lutz Mark (Eds), 1985, *Essays in Gandhian Economics,* Gandhi Peace Foundation, New Delhi.
10. Iyenger Sudershan 2005. "Sustainable Development and Indian Economy: Some Reflections", E.F. Schumacher Memorial Lecture delivered at the Nagpur University on February 5, 2005.
11. Lakdawal D.T. 1971. "Gandhiji and Growth Economic", in Raval M.N. et. al. (Eds.), *Gandhiji's Economic Thought and its Relevance at Present,* South Gujrat University, Surat.
12. Parel Anthony J. (Ed.) 1997. *Gandhi: Hind Swaraj and Other Writings,* Foundation Books, New Delhi for Cambridge University Press, U.K.
13. Raval M.N. 1971. "Contentment and Containment of Wants - A Suggested Interpretation", in Raval M.N. et al. (Eds), *Gandhiji's Economic Thought and its Relevance at Present,* South Gujrat University, Surat.
14. Sethi J. D. 1978. *Gandhi Today,* Vikas Publishing House Pvt. Ltd., New Delhi.
15. Siddharthan N.S. 1985. *The Gandhian Thought and the Information (Fourth Industrial) Revolution',* Indian Economic Association, Conference Volume, 68th Annual Conference, Ahmedabad

Life Agalinst Good Life :
The Need for Reflection

Ramashray Roy

"If you dwell on the past, you lose one of your eyes; if you forget the past, you lose both your eyes". –A Russian Proverb

The incompatibility between "life" and the "good life", as the title implies, refers to two modes of man's existence. If the term "life" refers to a life devoted of the satisfaction of ordinary life needs, the term "good life" underlines the need for every man to grow to the full stature of humanity, the seeds of which are implanted deep in the being. This does not by any means signify the negation of the basic concerns of the pragmatic dimensions of existence. It only means to be alive to the demands of the intellectual and spiritual aspects of life. Man's being in its totality is represented by a complex of body, mind, and spirit; it is necessary for every individual to cater to the needs of his total being. If, for any reason, one of these elements receives greater or fuller attention as compared to others, the holistic pattern of the development of man to the fullest extent of his potentialities gets distorted. This distortion affects not only his internal psychic balance but also the pattern of his relationship with the external world, both society and nature.

The danger of distortion, both internally in man's psyche and externally in his relationship with the external world, looms large then what if a harmonious continuity is transformed, both conceptually and existentially, into antagonistic dichotomy. The consequence that flows out of this dichotomy is also the positing of the orientation that treats them as mutually exclusive categories underscoring the belief that one cannot pursue both since they lack compatibility. In effect, this amounts to insisting that the celebration of life with a view to paving the way for a comfortable life or a life that enjoys all the "relishes" that the development of the material aspect of man's existence can supply with ease, must not be eclipsed by a tilt towards the pursuit of good life. This means that the goals of life and that of good life are not only different, they are also incompatible and, perhaps, antagonistic. If the goal of life aims at the acquisition of wealth, power and prestige, the goal of pursuing a mode of life that aims at actualizing the full potential incorporating not only biological but also intellectual and spiritual potentialities must be given up.

It in this context we can appreciate the posited antagonism between life and good life. For example, the famous Hindi poet Rahim underlines that: *Rahiman gali hai sankari, dono nahi raha nhi, Ham ahain to Hari nahi, Hari to apun nahi* (Rahiman says that the lane is quite narrow, it cannot accommodate both Hari (God) and aap (the sense of ego). If there abides the sense of ego, God will not stay there and if it is occupied by God, the sense of ego must vacate it). Rahim does not talk of a life developed completely and single-mindedly to the acquisition of wealth, power and prestige, to be sure. The antagonism that he talks of refers to incompatibility between devotion to God and the sense of ego. But cannot the sense of ego be extended to incorporate the idea of devoting one's life to the service of fickle-minded Lakshmi with all her companions? A moment's deliberation would forcefully suggest that suggested that such an extension is possible. To make this extension successful, we have simply to ask a question. In what existential situation does the sense of ego emerge as the most dominant, if not exclusive, element in human existence? The answer to this question must not be sought in the inherent attributes of the ego itself but in an existential order in which some of the attributes of the ego assume utmost importance in contrast to others and become quite prominent in guiding man's destiny in this world of here and now.

The raising of this question draws our attention to the fact that the sense of ego (or as the Samkhya system of Indian philosophy calls it, *ahamkar*) happens to be just one of man's faculties and that in many existential situations, it lies dormant, overtly disciplined by higher faculties like *chitta* and *buddhi*. However, in certain propitious conditions, it throws off their harsh rule and gains autarchy. Only after it has gained some degree of independence from these higher faculties that ego or *ahamkar* undertakes to determine the way a person should interact with the external world. The propitious conditions paving the way for the ego or *ahamkar* to attain the status of the arbiter of human destiny are produced when the prevailing divinized order begins to crumble under the pressure of the growing tension between different poles of reality. The poles of reality have their origin in the differentiating consciousness of man as it impinges on his self-understanding. Man's self-understanding is always mediated through his understanding of his relationship with reality out there.

The 'reality out there' is not by any means homogeneous and undifferentiated. In its undifferentiated form the reality out there is characterized as cosmos which includes all beings, even the Being who is supposed to have or caused to have created it. In this cosmos, only the Being is considered by many, to be real, the only truth that matters. *Ekdam sadviprah vahudha vadanti* (Wise men always speak of one truth in different ways). And this truth is the transcendent being, the One. This One may, as Parmenides underlines, be transcendent, existent not in the world but beyond it. Or alternatively, it may be transcendent but immanent in the world, as the Vedas speaks of. In this form, the One becomes, through procession, the Many[(iv)]. As Yajurveda says, God created the world and then entered it[(v)]. Thus while in the Vedic perspective, the world, even though only the shadow or the reflection of the one, it is not unreal because as the Upanishad underlines, it is the residence of the Isha[(vi)]. Thus in the Vedic perspective, God is both transcendent and immanent and the world as his abode is real. In contrast to this, according to Parmenides, the real being is the transcendent being which is the ground of all other beings, to be true. However, everything other than the transcendent being has a secondary character or being an illusionary character. It is because of this that Parmenides distinguishes between real being as *aletheia*, being is truth, true reality, and secondary being as doxa, illusionary reality of opinion, secondary reality.

It needs to be stressed here that the distinction between aletheia and doxa does not in any way make a difference to reality which remains unaffected by the distinction that man makes. What this distinction refers to is a state of consciousness that has come to make this distinction as an aid to man's self-understanding. The consciousness which earlier posited an affinity with the 'reality out there' on the basis of identity and, therefore, did not make any distinction between the true and the unreal, the aletheia and the doxa has now come to make this differentiation. And in this differentiation, man's consciousness has itself undergone a process of differentiation. The process of the differentiation of man's consciousness begins with the making of a distinction between transcendence and immanence. Once this distinction is made, the way for making further distinctions opens. This becomes possible because of the equation that is established between real-unreal and existent-nonexistent[(vii)]. This equation underlines the fact that the real One is the only existent being who while transcendent is also immanent, present in all beings that he created. It is by virtue of this that the Being is existent although he does not exist in time and space.

Time and space are the extensions of the One who is beyond them and yet he exists because without him both time and space will disappear. However, one can argue that what does not exist in time and space does not exist because it is beyond the domain of experience. And since the One is beyond experience, it does not exist. If he does not exist, it cannot be said to have created or caused to be created the *idam sarvam* that we see all around you; it has evolved through the ages and subsists on its own. The experience of transcendence and immanence thus forms a triangle with three poles whose relationship defines one particular mode of self-consciousness in tension with the divine ground of reality. But this is just one mode of experience, a mode that recognizes God as the ground of reality; it is this recognition that influences man's relation with the external world. This relation, it needs to be emphasized, is permeated with the conscious awareness of God as the ground of being as well as the animator of man's experience. It is in this sense that Plato insists that things in this world become things because they participate in what in his view is the world-transcendent Idea.

In contrast to the Platonic construction, there is the Vedic construction which views beings as a part of the divine and therefore not separated from divine ground of reality as long as man does not get enveloped in the fog of ignorance or becomes indifferent to the God dwelling in the remotest corner of his heart. Because of the indwelling God, the psyche becomes the site of the conjunction of and interaction between the limited and the unlimited, the momentary and the timeless, the mortal and the immortal. In addition, the psyche is also the sensorial of the divine, that is, it is from here that the awareness that one is the part of divine or that one's psyche is the site in which the experience of immediacy under God, or the divine ground of one's own existence, pervades one's being[(viii)]. However, as pointed out earlier, consciousness differentiates over time and there comes a fateful distinction between actual participation and the awareness of participation. Once this distinction appears, it paves the way for reflective experience of the cosmos. The cosmos is now seen as having two segments, one with and the other without God.

Eventually, the segment with God too becomes a matter of critical examination. It is true that God in the segment with God is existent, but one cannot have a reliable knowledge of him. One cannot see God nor have any sensual experience of him. However, there are things in the world that one can view and experience as well. These things are real and the world that contains these things is by the same token, also real. The things that one can actually experience, it can be argued, constitute what is reality, they must be treated as reality, and everything else is not reality. As such there is no ground of being, there is no God. This represents a reconstruction of reality that is the polar antithesis of the one which is based on and derived from a conscious recognition of the divine ground of reality. What now happens is that with the rejection of the divine ground of reality whose experience constitutes one mode of consciousness is given up in favour of another reconstruction that is inspired by the idea of a de-divinized world. But this does not mean that God has disappeared from man's consciousness. However, the experience of the de-divinized world has given rise to a new conception of humanity which is radically different from, even opposed to, the one that is derived from the conscious and living awareness of the divine ground of reality.

When viewed from the perspective of a well differentiated consciousness, the cosmos now splits into a tripartite arrangement that describes a triangle of the divine, the mankind and the world. And since mankind as a generic term is understandable in terms of the notion of humanity only, the meaning of humanity will differ according to the kind of relationship one posits or is seen to exist between all aspects of reality. Thus, the mere enunciation of who man is, is not enough a ground for defining humanity. This is so because man is not alone nor sufficient in himself. He lives in a structured or a sedimented world in which his location is defined in terms of his relationship with all other elements of reality. This humanity must be understood in the sense of man in a certain manner in relation to all other elements of reality. Humanity must be distinguished from the nature of man that is supposed to be stable;[ix] the conception of humanity will change if man's relationship with all the other elements of reality is viewed in different ways. Given this, we can define humanity, following Voegelin, as meaning 'man in a mode of understanding himself in his relation to God, world and society.'[x] And understandably, this mode changes over time in history.

Defined this way, humanity cannot be understood apart from the three absolute ideas that constitute the whole of reality. These absolute ideas are: universal divinity, universal humanity, and the universal idea of the world. When man is understood as an entity in tension with the divine ground of reality, then the universal idea of humanity emerges. This universal idea of humanity has its *raison d'etre* in the universal idea of divinity under which all men live. They become man by their presence under universal divinity. Then the rest of the world is shared by all; this is a world that is common to all.[xi] This common world is something that is analytically separated from man and divinity. When these three universal ideas -- universal divinity, universal humanity, and the universal world - are in balance, there emerges a particular kind of reality. What also needs to be mentioned in this connection is that when these three universals exhibit harmonious balance, a perfect order, an order that is characterized by a complete compatibility between the interior and the exterior of man, emerges. Such an order becomes the basis of homonia, that is, harmony as the result of man's participation in the common ground as Aristotle notes. When homonia prevails, every man is ordered in orientation towards that common ground, the nous. And it is this relationship between men that constitutes the order of society. Thus, the orientation towards the common ground yields common reason, paving the way for like-mindedness.

The origin in the experience of transcendence, of the immediacy of all men under God, as the source of common humanity is, for one reason or the other, destroyed, the balance between the three poles of reality - the universal divinity, the universal humanity, and the universal world - is also disturbed and distorted. These three universals represent a unit and it any one of them undergoes changes, that is, if it is perceived differently, then the whole apparatus of ideas which is inherent in the experience of man, the system of all the universals as a unit collapses. What we then get is a corrupted system in which one of the universals is made the centre of the system and the others become dependent upon it. Note, for example, that if the universal idea of humanity undergoes change as a result of the destruction of idea of origin in the experience of transcendence, the universal idea of man is replaced by some other idea of man. But this idea does not represent the whole of man; what happens is that some partial idea of man, for example, economic man, religious man, man the proletariat, etc. is hypostasized, and what happens is that some partial ideas of man, or fragmented ideas of man are picked up and we then attribute to them the quality of being universal. When the partial idea of man is hypostatized, the two other universal ideas become the function of man.

This also is true of the other two universal ideas. Note, for example, that if the universal divinity is absolutized, we have what Kabir project as the central theme of his message: *"Kabira Khada bazaar men, liye luhathi hath, Jo garh jare apne, chale hamare sath"*. (That is: Kabir is standing in the centre of the bazaar with a torch in his hand, one who wants to accompany him [in his journey to realize the God] must burn his house). What is distinctive about this message is that man becomes man only if he engages in the search of the absolute, the world is simply a stumbling block in this quest. If, on the other hand, the universal world is absolutized, man becomes a function of the world, and God becomes the function of man. This simply means that when a part of reality is treated as the absolute, the other parts are no longer credited with being real; they become dependent upon the part that has been absolutized. When this happens it does not mean that the reality as consisting of the three poles of reality in perfect balance has been obliterated, it only means that while reality goes on to exist just as it did before, man's consciousness of this reality has undergone a radical change and it now constructs the image of man as totally defined by the one universal idea that has been absolutized.

Once the balance between the three universals comes to be distorted, there is then the beginning of a new order, both within man's being and without, that redefines the relationship between these three universals. What is necessary to note here is that since humanity is defined in terms of man's self-understanding in relation to God, world and society, it gives rise to self-understanding of man that is grounded in his immediacy under God, that is if man's life and activities reflected a conscious recognition of the divine ground of reality, it produces a type of order within man's psyche as well as in the external world in which man's different faculties - body, mind and soul or intelligence, energy and appetites are in a stable, salubrious relationship with each other. This is also the case with respect of man, society and nature. Such an order is conducive to man's autonomy since he is not under the suzerainty of his passions but under the rule of the indwelling God. And since he is autonomous (*swarat*) as well as conscious of all other beings in the world as animated by and reflecting the same divine vital force, he becomes capable of transcending the pettiness of passion and desires and the soul-killing effect of self-interest Man becomes conscious of the fact that it is necessary to safeguard the essential integrity of all beings.

For, once man is in touch with his highest, he is in touch with God. He has then a broader and higher vision of man and his place in nature, and so he identifies himself with God and finds that he has no special interest of his own to serve. The low and the high, the sinful and the virtuous, are the same in his eyes, he perceives God in all things and all things in God.[xii]

Anchoring in God enables man to attain the virtue of *samatva* (sameness), that is, oneness of life. And it needs to be emphasized; the fountainhead of *samatva* is what Haractitus calls *xynon* (the shareable commonality). Without, this shareable commonality, homonoia is hard to conceive; and if there is no homonoia, there cannot be what Aristotle calls *philia politike* or love among men in a community. And if homonoia is destroyed, the order in society reflecting *philia politike* is disrupted. Once this happens, man becomes ego-centric and is always on the lookout for gaining freedom from the pressures of his environing society. The search for autonomy does not in any way signify the autonomy one enjoys or can enjoy as a result of man's immediacy under God, the divine ground of reality. On the contrary, autonomy now connotes man's ability to define his own life purposes and to find appropriate ways and means of realizing them. This at once makes it clear that characterizes certain ends worthy of pursuit and certain others as unworthy of man's attention or on agreement among individuals. Every individual has his own end to pursue without taking into account whether the end he proposes to pursue has benign or malignant consequences for others.

Once autonomy in the latter sense becomes the converted goal and live experience, the sense of *xynon* that lies buried in the interior of every individual is deadened. While *xynon* remains active or is actively acknowledged, man remains awake as Heracitus puts it, aware to his essential relatedness with his maker and to his destiny. 'Only one cosmos.... exists for the "waking" along, while the "sleepers" each have their own private world, a world of dreams.'[xiii] Propelled by the personal world of dream, the individual wakes up only when he thinks of thyself and plans to pursue the demands of the self immersed in materiality in competition with others, The goal of this competition is to acquire more and more goodies of this world with a view to satisfy the demands of his world of dream. This is symptomatic of man's total immersion in the pursuit of self-interest that emerges as a central concern after the individual joins the rank of the 'sleepers'. The centrality of the pursuit of interest reduces society and nature to the status of potential means for the realization of individual purposes. In addition, reason is transformed into calculative, expediential reasoning and concerns for higher quantity of goods and services escalate. But their satisfaction becomes more and more difficult. As expectations from the external world mount, dissatisfaction and disillusionment also go on increasing. As a result, human existence gets denuded of all meanings leading to anomie, apathy, and, not infrequently, rebellion.

It is the apprehension of such a human condition, a condition pregnant with the dangers of disarray adversely affecting individual wellbeing and social concord, that constituted the central concern of traditional thinking not only in India but also elsewhere. The principal motif of traditional thinking is the maintenance of the balance between the three universals discussed above. It is this balance that, in the traditional perspective, ensures individual wellbeing and social concord. The main threat to individual wellbeing and social concord is, in the traditional mode of thinking, posed by the natural man and his doings in a situation where individual worlds of dream conflict with each other and destroys the basis of *philia politike.* Herein we can see the irresistible impetus for life to pose a severe threat to the possibility of good life. This state of affairs can be prevented from appearing if the divided that separates the natural man from the world around him could be eliminated. This is possible only when the conscious energy and purpose that surround the world are considered to be forging an organic system. In this organic system, the cosmos symbolizes a metabolism of which the structure of interdependence and exchange of mutually supportive and sustaining process of exchange of gifts and benefits constitute essential characteristics.[xiv] It is this process of exchange that establishes firmly a *quatenarian* community of *martya, amartya, prithiwi and dyau* or, as Plato puts it in *Gorgias* differently, of man and God and society and the world. As long as this community subsists, self-transformation remains within the realm of possibility.

What is of vital importance in these quaternaries primordial community is transcendence, particularly the transcendence of the empirical self associated with what is usually characterized as the natural man. Self-transcendence signifies in the context a process directed at installing the soul, the seat and the sensorial of divine, as the ruler over all other psychic forces. This facilitates the quelling of the rebellion of appetites and passions. When they are controlled and confined, reason is released from its bondage to desires. Man is then able to rise above the contingencies of individual existence and can attune his soul to the One who underlies as well as pervades the bewildering diversity of the phenomenal world. Reason in love with and attuned to the One constitutes the basis for identity with and active love for the beings in the world. This, needless to say, is what is basic to the *Upanishadic* view that insists on the oneness of everything, sensate and insensate. The *adhyatmam-adhidaivik-adhibhautik* system(xv) posits, a thoroughgoing scheme of correspondence between the subjective and the objective and considers all the three as different aspects of one sole imperishable entity, known respectively from the subjective and objective points of view.

The perspective delineated above is well brought out in the traditional mode of thinking. This can very well be elucidated from three perspectives from the past. These perspectives refer to thought-ways expressed in two different and distinct cultures, the Hellenic and the Vedic. We analyze here two perspectives from Hellas, Aristotle and Plato, and then focus on the Vedic perspective from India. What is interesting to note in this connection is that each of these perspectives identifies the love for life, in the sense of what Mahatma Gandhi calls the search for "bodily comfort" as the enemy of the soul. Referring to the hypocrisy of modern civilization,(xvi) he likens it with "a wolf through its hunger for wealth and its greedy pursuit of worldly pleasures."(xvii) The propelling force of modern civilization symbolizing the celebration of life is what he calls 'the hunger for wealth and greedy pursuit of worldly pleasures.' Lying at the core of modern civilization, the craving for the augmentation of fortunes has profoundly influenced the life of the individual. As a result, the individual thinks of nothing else and devotes his whole energy to assessing and increasing wealth for adding to bodily comforts. This is symptomatic of the sickness of the soul. It is this sickness that spreads out and reappears as the symptoms of a diseased social order which tolerates, nay, encourages, inequality, intolerance, exploitation, and oppression.

It is this state's of affairs that constitutes the point of departure for each of these perspectives to ponder and propose the way out of the existential malaise the love for life in the material sense brings in its train. One can raise the question why should one go back to the past to get inspiration for mending the disorder prevailing in the present. What is past is dead and gone; as such, what is the use of flogging a dead horse. No matter how much of flogging it receives, it is never going to move. Moreover, what the past signifies is simply ignorance, superstition and dogma. The rise of science has successfully cut to the heart of the fog of ignorance that that past has spread all around. The past epitomizes ignorance and, therefore, anti-rationality. In addition, time never stands still, if marches on and in its movement forward, it lets loose a stream of changes. These changes also affect society which never retains uniformity in the movement of time. As such, how could something that happened in the time past be a guide for what is troubling mankind today? During the course of change, problems change, along with these changes, circumstances too change. The solutions that might have been useful in the distant past have certainly lost their relevance and efficacy in the present. Also, the past is simply a memory, scratches on our mind, merely the pointer to what happened long ago. In view of all this, we must conclude that the past has little or no relevance for the present.

But has the past lost all its relevance and salience for the present? It is true the past has been completely eclipsed by the advent of the modern. The advent of the modern also has signaled the pre-eminence of linear conception of time replacing the circular conception. The linear connection of time posits the idea of endless progression of history in which all points of time constitute a straight line with each point being superseded by the following point. In this conception of time, past has no relevance for the present. It is this conception of time that is regnant in the Western thinking. The past, in this thinking, is meaningful either as the womb of the present or the necessary condition for the emergence of the present. What is also noteworthy in this connection is the fact that when the present is viewed from a distance of objectivity it always seems to be full of trouble. As a result, the future is always viewed as something that is better, peaceful and well ordered -The opposition of a dead past through a present into a future which is always conceived to be better, pregnant with the possibility of redemption of mankind. The conception of future signifies a meaning of the term "future" which does not come into currency before the middle of the 18th century, at least in the Western tradition of thinking. This conception of time is grounded in a view of history which posits the idea of perfection of man and his environing social order lying somewhere in the indefinite future. One of those who propound this view of history is, of course, Immanuel Kant who sees man progressing from the state of barbarism through several intervening stages to ultimately a perfectly better, peaceful and harmonious future. For Kant, history is, then, an indefinite approach to the realm of perfection.

The fact, however, stands out that such a future recedes into an indefinite future which never makes its appearance. As such, the hope of man's perfection ever hangs on a thin and treacherous thread of hollow promise. Such a view of history also negates the divine and its movement on the ever-moving scale of time. In contradistinction to this, there is an alternative conception of history in which past is ever living in relation to the present. If, as T.S. Elliot puts it, every point in the movement of time represents the point of intersection of time with the timeless, then, our own location on any point of the movement of time symbolizes our openness towards divine reality. Every point in the movement of time is the point of presence. Thus, the whole series of time would not be a series on a line at all, but only a series of present points in which none is ever past, but only past in relation to their present, and not really past. If this were not so, there is no reason to remember whatever happened three thousand years ago or only three minutes ago, unless there was a reason perhaps to remember it, because it is connected without present point. As such, the movement of time and the idea of change in history must be treated as something like a flow of presence, a few in which there is permanently a tension between the immanent and transcendent poles of existence. It is this tension in the flow of presence that traditional thinking is concerned with. Also, it is for this reason those different modes of the perception of this tension and a possible resolution of the conflicts deriving from this tension that pervade human consciousness, are relevant for the present and its troubles.

Having taken care of the objection to the salience of the past for the present, we must return now to discussing what the three perspectives from the past have to other pertaining to what Mahatma Gandhi identified as the cause of the eclipse of the good life by life.

What is of importance in this connection is the very conception of the good life that these perspectives from the past hold. The meaning of the good life for each of these perspectives from the past hold the meaning of the life for each of these perspectives consists in safeguarding the integrity of the primordial community, the community formed by God and man, world and society. This primordial community is simply a possibility; it has not yet become real in the true sense of the term. It can be safeguarded only when man becomes the intersection of time with the timeless; that is, when man attunes his soul to the divine ground of reality. Such an attunement links the finite with the Infinite, the Absolute, and calls upon man to prove worthy of this linkage by letting his orientation and behaviour be moulded by satisfying the conditions in which this linkage becomes meaningful. To put it differently, it is this linkage that must become the source of meaning, truth, and value. Only when this linkage moulds the total being of man, the possibility of the good life becomes real. It is this conception of the good life that each of these perspectives from the past celebrates.

For example, take Plato's conception of the good life. In his *Republic*, the most important dialogue of Plato is the one where he is concerned with the moral and political question of what justice is; it is in this context that such questions as 'what is the basis of social and moral obligation', 'Why should one become law-abiding or moral', or 'why should a person become good' become relevant. It does not need to be emphasized that these questions go to the heart of yet another vitally important question: 'How is justice served in a city?' Plato's approach to this question, needless to say, is anthropological. This signifies that he establishes a homology between man and the polity when he says that polis is man writ large. As such, the kind of life pattern that is good and preferable can very well be discerned from the consideration of what is the best form of government. This demands from Plato a convincing delineation of what the good life consists of. In explicating what good life is, Socrates, the mouthpiece of Plato, when convinced of the futility of dialectical reasoning in demonstrating what justice is, adopts in *Republic* II, 368-371 the strategy of showing justice in the 'whole city',[xviii] and in this process creates first a simple city, a city that can cater nothing more than the subsistence needs or plain necessities of its population Glaucon characterizes this city as only fit for pigs[xix] and argues that it is not a true city since it does not provide for relish for a person like Glaucon nor does it accommodate those who are blessed with spiritedness. He then asks for constructing the model of a city that can provide the wherewithal of an elegant life.

According to Glaucon's demand, Socrates argues that if a city conforming to Glaucon's idea is constructed, it will substantively mean that the city must provide for 'the supplement to the indispensable staples of human life. 'In effect, it means "the inclusion of the full array of goods and services commonly accepted as pertaining to an elegant life style.'[xx] Clearly, then, if the city is organized to serve the demands of an elegant lifestyle, it must admit a multiplicity of goods and services requiring a very large number of specialists who must be trained and recruited to service limitless appetites. The city will inevitably grow in size; it will have a greatly enlarged community; it will be swollen up with a whole multitude of callings not ministering to only bare necessity.[xxi] With the increase in the size of the community, the territory which was large enough to support a small population proves too small to support a large population. As a result, 'we shall have to cut off a slice of our neighbour's territory' and if they too are not content with bare necessaries. ;They will want a slice of ours.' This will inevitably end in war.[xxii] War will necessitate a big standing army. Also, this will require specialization and division of labour. It means that men engaged in different occupations necessary for providing goods and services for endlessly proliferating needs must be equipped with the greatest amount of skill and practice.[xxiii] This is also true of those who are to guide and rule over the destiny of the polis.

In becoming large, the city is in no condition to exclude any good or service as long as it is technologically possible to provide them. This signifies that the polis lacks a basis to discriminate between appetites; in want of such a discriminatory standard, all desires will carry equal weight. It also means that there is, consequently, no longer a hierarchy among the myriad of goods and services that the city permits. 'Like the inflamed appetites it is obliged to admit, the city is itself limitless. It possesses yet no principle according to which its order or even its completion may be determined.'[xxiv]

When the state lacks completeness, it lacks justice too. Thus, Glaucon's demand for relish produces nothing more than a promiscuous heap, stuffed and multitudinous.(xxv) The fact that the city has grown large does not mean that it is a well-integrated political community, or it has become whole in the sense of reflecting civic wholeness. As a matter of fact, in want of civic wholeness, diversity or, to put it in its contemporary usage, pluralism, poses a threat to the viability and vitality of the polis inasmuch as it promotes particularism and self-aggrandizement (*pleonexia*) rooted in self-love. In such a situation, what is there to keep the watchdogs of the polis from turning into wolf and devouring their fellow citizens? Also, the polis, when facing a crisis, will find very few citizens to defend it against the ruler's abuse of power.

It is clear, then, that the polis does not become whole or complete by allowing unrestricted increase of goods and services. The wholeness evidently depends instead upon the establishment of a principled relationship among the diverse parts of the polis. Plato calls this principle *politeia*. The search and installation of politeia requires. Plato argues, to overcome and transcend what he calls "cognitive bewitchment" induced by the needs and appetites of the body.(xxvi) To quote Plato:

For the body is the source of endless trouble to us by reason of the mere requirement of food... and by filling up as full of loves, and lusts, and fears, and fancies, and idols, and every sort of folly, prevents our ever having, as people say, so much as a thought. For whence come wars, and fighting, and factions? Whence but from the body and the lust of the body.(xxvii)

It is this lust of the body that makes man the slave of many mad masters and unless the soul "escapes from the servitude of many mad masters,"(xxviii) there is justice neither in the interior of man nor in the polis. As long as man is engrossed in an appetitive life, it is difficult for him to apprehend truth. Seeing the true and the good is possible only through the soul's eye.(xxix) However, the soul is buried deep down in "some barbaric slime,"(xxx) and cannot see clearly. It is therefore necessary to train the mind to develop the capacity of putting particulars together to realize the single idea behind them. It is what Plato calls "synoptic vision". It is possible when the soul turns round (perigee) from the world of appearance towards the source of light that makes the eye of the soul to see, distinguish between what is only apparently good and what is really good. As the sun is the source of light in the physical universe, so is the idea of God the source of truth and meaning in the social world. And the idea of Good can be grasped only when the soul is rescued through perigee from its bondage too appetites and is attuned to the divine ground of being which is the source of the true and the good.(xxxi) When "the eye of the soul" is fixed on the Good, it yields the knowledge or the synoptic vision with the help of which one can perceive the patterning of right ordering. This is true both in the case of the individual and the polis.(xxxii)

In so far as the question of right ordering is concerned. Socrates suggests a hierarchy of values reflecting a clearly graduated theory of goods, which places spiritual good the highest, physical goods below them, and external goods like property and power in the lowest place.(xxxiii) Plato too imposes a hierarchy on goods which treats they should as the divine in man; it is the locus of intelligence through which the divine ground of being can be apprehended. And since it constitutes the divine part of man, the soul must rule over spiritedness and appetites. It is, therefore, man's primary responsibility to care for his soul; it is only on this basis that man's quest for knowledge of values and of truth, prognosis and *aletheia*, can come to fruition. In short, only on the basis of prognosis and *aletheia* that the vision of Agathon that forms should through the experience of transcendence is possible. It is this that makes it possible to put one's interior in order by installing the soul as the sensorium of divine, that is, as the ruler over other facilities.(xxxiv)

Installation of the soul as the ruler in man's interior signifies the adoption of a way of life, bios in the true sense of the term. The soul, when properly trained, becomes the locus of *sophia* (wisdom) which, in turn, represents a particular ethical code. It is this ethical code by which, in turn, represents a particular ethical code. It is this ethical code by which man can organize his life activities. Living by such a code man develops the capacity to resist nature and attains eudemonia, perfect happiness. This underlines the fact that '... man cannot reach happiness with being through the cultivation and satisfaction of his own senses and his bodily nature... but only through complete mastery over himself in accordance with the law he finds by searching his own soul."[xxxv] To live under the suzerainty of the soul, the soul that is attuned to the divine ground of reality, and to follow an ethical code derived from this attunement is, for Plato, good life.

Like Plato, Aristotle, too, argues for transcending the lure of what Plato has called external goods like wealth and power for living a good life. According to Aristotle, there are three types of life: the apaulistic life, that is, life given to hedonistic indulgences; the political life, that is, *vita activa*, underlining participation in and active involvement with the management of public affairs; and bios theoreticos, that is, the life given to contemplation.[xxxvi] Each of these types of life has its own *eudaimonia*, that is to say, pleasure for the vulgar type, that is for 'the mass of mankind (who) are evidently quite slavish in their tastes, preferring a life suitable to beasts.' Similarly, the end of political life is seeking honour and doing noble deeds, while the life of contemplation pursues the end of virtue. Accordingly, there are corresponding virtues: pleasure, *phronesis* and *sophia*.[xxxvii] Aristotle rejects the life of pleasure because it is irrational, on one hand, and it tends to lead to *pleonexia*, on the other. Pleonexia means, at one and the same time, two things: one, it shows the tendency to act so as to aggrandize oneself, whether one's deserts entitle one to it or not and, two, to act so as to suffer injustice voluntarily.[xxxviii]

For Aristotle, then, the *apaulistic* life, the life of pleasure, stands at the lowest rung of the hierarchy of values. It is true that the life of contemplation, *bios theoreticos* is to be preferred as the highest good, but it is not possible for all to engage in the pursuit of such a life. As such, political life, *vita activa*, becomes the lot of the mass of the people. *Vita activa* signifies a life lived in a community or a state where men share some common interests. For Aristotle the state is natural and represents a natural association as against partial associations of the family and the village. It is a perfect association because it encompasses not only the totality of man's being but also because it is only the state that makes it possible for all to live a good life. Good life, Aristotle insists, is the chief end, both for the community as a whole and for each of us individually. But men also come together and form and maintain political association merely for the sake of life; for perhaps there is some element of good even in the simple act of living, so long as the evils of existence to not preponderate too heavily.[xxxix]

It is clear that what Aristotle has in mind is what Charles Taylor calls a two-tier view of human purposes.[xl] On the one side, there are ordinary life needs that must be fulfilled for the sake of life; on the other side, there are higher purposes which must be given effect to if life has to have some meaning and value, that is, the good life. The former is what Aristotle called the realm of necessity and the latter signifies the realm of freedom. And for a meaningful good life, it is necessary to make a transition from the realm of necessity to that of freedom. Without such a transition, the evils of existence are most likely to corrupt human existence. A life given simply to the fulfillment of ordinary life needs involved with production and reproduction has as its end pleasure, however, such a life is irrational because it does not respond or even harkens to and accept the claim of certain rationally determined ends. In this sense, it is a life which is, to use Cooper's term, "open-ended" it is open-ended in the sense that It bids us to maximize in our lives as a whole the amount of a certain good, but without specifying at all what this maximum may be. It leaves it entirely up to us, in principle at any rate, to alter our mode of life in adjustment to changing circumstances and altered capacities for enjoyment as our lives themselves develop. There are no fixed principles of living, though of course there may be a variety of experience of the common situations of life and the pleasure or pain that usually issues from various courses of action taken in them. Such rules are only rules of thumb, however, and not fixed principles.[xli]

It is clear then, that *apaulistic* life or the life of pleasure, is without principles and a life without principles is rudderless, flowing aimlessly on the sea of unbounded desires. *Apaulistic* life is not possible if one has no access to unlimited wealth. Aristotle makes a distinction between natural wealth and unnatural wealth. By natural wealth he means the acquisition of wealth drawn directly from nature, such as, farming, hunting, etc.[xlii] and exchange of goods for the satisfaction of needs rather than profit. These modes of acquiring wealth are treated by Aristotle as natural. There is also another way of acquiring wealth which is aimed at earning profit. This becomes possible only after the introduction of coins as something that facilitate the exchange of commodities through trade and commerce. The wealth so acquired is not so much for consumption as for accumulation. Wealth so acquired is treated by Aristotle as unnatural.(xliii) But why does a person become motivated to acquire more and more of wealth? Aristotle argues that some people become eager for life; they want to make the span of their life as long as possible. And since the desire for life is unlimited, desire for riches also becomes unlimited. The origin of the disposition to acquire more and more wealth lies, as Aristotle observes, in the fact that they are intent upon living only and not upon living well; and, as their desires are unlimited, 'they also desire that the means of gratifying them should be without limit'.(xliv)

It is true that even those who aim at good life seek the means of obtaining bodily pleasures; and since the enjoyment of these pleasures appears to depend on wealth, they are absorbed in making money. However, there is a fundamental difference between the disposition of those who aim at good life and who those who believe only in living well. While those who believe in the former live according to a fixed principle of living, they do not acquire wealth for the sake of wealthy, but only as a means to satisfying bodily needs; in contrast, those who believe in living aim at excessive enjoyment and, therefore, if they 'are not able to supply their pleasures by the art of money-making, they try other arts, using in turn every faculty in a manner contrary to nature'.(xlv) Such persons think pleasure as the end of life and yoke everything at their disposal to serve this end. What is irksome to Aristotle is the excess in doing anything. The *apaulistic* life itself testifies to the fact that those who aim at living indulge in excess insofar as the acquisition of wealth and property is concerned.

Aristotle advocates moderation with a view to avoiding the evil consequences of excesses. He is convinced that an *apaulistic* life leads to the phenomenon of *pleonexia*. And *phronesis*, practical reason, underlines the need to avoid *pleonexia* since it proves vicious not only for the individual but also for the social order. To act virtuously is, therefore, to act in accordance with a mean, a middle state between two extremes, this is moderation, temperance. Moderation is the distinctive feature of a person who is blessed with two characteristics. First, such a person is capable of controlling his passions. In a moderate man, passions are expected to be in harmony with other parts of his being, especially his reason; second, he must develop the capacity to resist tyranny, that is the adverse consequences of someone's action for others, on the one hand, and willful violation of justice, on the other. A moderate person is thus committed to the end of the good life, that is, to suppress and curb the excesses that are inherent in life as against good life.

As we have seen in the case of two prominent thinkers of Hellas. Plato and Aristotle, both of them underline the necessity of overcoming the lust for life and cultivating good life by transiting from the realm of necessity to the realm of freedom. The need to transcend the demands of mere life and to aim at the realization of the end of the good life is also the central theme of the Vedic philosophy. To begin the discussion of this aspect of the Vedic philosophy we must begin with the myth of Vritra. In Rigveda X 124.6 there is expressed the need to kill Vritra (*Hanava Vritram*). But who is this Vritra and why does there arise the need to kill him? It turns out that Vritra is someone who has obstructed successfully the process of creation. In the Vedic likely story of creation, or cosmogony, Agni lies in the womb of *apah*; as long as he does not become manifest, the process of creation cannot move ahead. But the manifestation of Agni is obstructed by what in the Vedic cosmogonic account is called Vritra,[(xlvi)] who must be killed to let Agni be born.

The removal of Vritra was seen to be a difficult task because Agni, Soma, Dyava and Prithiwi, all of them had been absorbed by Vritra. As a result, he had become very powerful. Finally, Indra was given the responsibility of killing Vritra. When Indra challenged *Vritra*, he fled but could not stop the desertion of Agni, Soma, Dyava and Prithiwi, who when invited by Indra to join his rank, did so. This rendered Vritra very weak and Indra, when he caught up with him, hurled his vajra at Vritra who fell down having been seriously wounded. When Indra was ready to deal him a death blow,

Vritra requests him to stop. Indra does so and was told by Vritra that if he killed Vritra, Indra himself will be destroyed in as much as all the strength that had accrued to him was due to the fact that Agni, Soma, Dyava and Prithiwi had now become a part of his being while earlier they were with Vritra. Indra was therefore requested to cut him into two parts without killing him. Indra did so; one part of Vritra that was benign became the moon and the other malignant part entered different creatures as their belly. As a result, all creatures began since then to experience the pangs of hunger (*ashanaya*). And hunger is one thing that drives men to commit sin.

It is true that the strong element of *ashanaya* in every being prompts it to commit sin. However, this tendency can be checked if man remembers that he is the abode of the absolute. In the Vedic perspective, it is the Gods who brought together the things and poured into the mortal the juice of life; having done so, they entered man. Thus, the Gods made the mortal their abode and then entered into it.[(xlvii)] It is clear, then, that everything in this universe is Brahma's breath or, to use another metaphor, the sparks of the Divine Fire[(xlviii)] (*yathagne ksudra visphullinga vyucharanti*). And despite the fact that human beings are integral parts of the Divine, their identity with the Divine source is not total. And as long as it is not total, the human person will not be perfect, he will, as a consequence, lack harmony.[(xlix)] In the lack of harmony, the absolute is covered by five sheaths, four of which constitute the source of error.[(l)] Of the five essences the absolute possesses, eternity is circumscribed by *kala* (time), all permanence by determination (*niyati*), plenitude by desire (raga), omniscience by intellect (*buddhi*) and omnipotence by limited capacity.[(li)] Once these four sheaths lead a person to error, the absolute abiding in the human heart, which is identified by Rigveda VII.86.6 as the elder brother or as *sakshi suparna* (the witness) by Dirghatamas,[(lii)] is usually ignored by the mortal (younger brother of the Rigveda VII.86.6 and *bhoktiri suparna* (person who enjoys the fruits of his action). It is true that the elder brother stays with the younger brother, however, (*asti jyayam kaniyas upare*, Rigveda VII. 86.6), he is not often acknowledged except in the time of trouble when the younger brother cannot find any other anchor, support or help. He does not desert him who is nearby, but he does not see Him who is so close to him (*astiantam na jahayanti santam no pashyati*).[(liii)]

This points to the bivalent nature of man with the inherent possibility of his going one way or the other. As Kathopanishad I.III.3 underlines: The chariot of this body of man has in him the *amartya* (the immortal) as the master of this chariot, the intellect as the charioteer, and mind as the bridge. In this chariot, senses (*indriyas*) are like horses which have objects as their way. It is only when the Inner Dweller is actively associated with the body, senses and mind that the chariot of human body moves well and ensures its own wellbeing. But the trouble is that Swayambhoo created the senses, to be sure; however, they were damaged in the process of being created and, therefore, they can see only the outer things, not the Divine Being within (*paranchi khani vyatrinat swaymbhoostasmat parangposhyati nantaratman*, Kathopanishad II.I.I). When the senses look out, they see a multiplicity of objects and get entrapped in them. And since they become attached to these objects, they get immersed in materiality. Driven by the willful horses of the senses, the indwelling *amartya* gets caught up in the same sense of pleasure and pain.[(liv)] And then there is no cessation of pleasure and pain. As a consequence, a person becomes *kamachara* (a person who is moved by the disposition to realize his desires). And as a *kamachara* he must become *arthasamgrahi* (one who goes an acquiring the means of satisfying desires, i.e. acquisition of more and more wealth).

A *kamachara* is deserted by God. He does not become the friend of those who become acquisitive and possessive (*naki revantam sakhyaya vindase*) because those who are puffed up with wine offends him (*piyantgi te suraswah*, Rigveda VIII.21.14).[(lv)] And one who offends the absolute residing in his interior, the natural man, becomes spiritually blind.[(lvi)] This is why he cannot make a distinction between the sun whom everyone sees and the sun which not all know with the mind (*pashyanti sarve chakshusha no sarve manasa vida*, Atharvaveda X.9.14). As a result, the senses, when not associated with the indwelling God, become attached to external objects with the result that man becomes covetous. And 'he who covets the desirable things while brooding (on their virtues), is born amidst those very surroundings along with his desires.[(lvii)] A covetous man disrupts the yajna (sacrifice) that always goes on at all levels of cosmic hierarchy. In so far as this yajna at the personal level is concerned, it is for self-transformation. It is the continuous process of self-transformation that becomes instrumental in the preservation of the cosmic order by safeguarding the process of exchange between man, God and other beings. This process is disrupted by coveting more than what one needs for the preservation of life invites death.[lviii] He destroys the bridge of humanity and becomes the cause of disorder both within his own interior and within the social order.

Our survey of the perspectives from the past on man and his world, forcefully brings to the fore the incompatibility between life and good life. If man is engrossed in the affairs of this world, he then precludes the possibility of attaining the end of the good life. Once the end of the good life is discarded or pushed into the background, man becomes what *Chhandogya Upanishad* calls *anyarata*, the slave of his desires. His slavery to desires induces acute internal disorder which manifests as disorder in the external world, especially, the social world. Once society becomes diseased, it denudes the possibility of a person getting out of the disorder that threatens to absorb his whole being. When internal order is matched by disorder in society, every man is forced to live an alienated life. Structures of social cooperation and interdependence dissolve, and the tendency of beggar they neighbour becomes deep rooted. It is these factors that lie at the root of modern problematic. This problematic has spread its tentacles everywhere and has closed all avenues of release. The modern times exhibit it amply.

The advent of modern times has radically changed the self-consciousness of man vis-a-vis God, society and the world. The character of self-consciousness, needless to say, differs both in texture, tone and content from what it was in the past. As our survey of the three perspectives from the past suggests, man's self-consciousness was then expansive in the sense that it was grounded in an understanding that treated the cosmos as exemplifying a quaternaries primordial community in which man was not considered to be self-complete and self-sufficient, he was just one segment, although a very important one, of the cosmos and he shared with other segments a commonality and constituted simply a link in the chain of exchange between *martya-amartya* and *Prithiwi-Dyau*. It was this exchange process that preserved and safeguarded the unity and continuity of the cosmos. With the coming of the modern times, all this changed. Man's self-understanding went through a radical transformation; he reduced himself to his empirical self that it, his ego and his activities revolved round his ego-activities. God lost his relevance; society came to be considered only a potential means for the realization of man's purpose, and the world that was traditionally to be a common world came now to be separately shared. With these changes, man's self-image changed; he treated himself the lord and master of the world but came instead to be a function of the world. Even though man becomes extremely dependent on the world, he still considers himself, in the modern times, a free agent who obeys the demands of his own nature unrestrained by any authority external to himself. It is this development that lies at the root of the modern problematic; this development describes a radical shift from the spiritual pole to the material pole of man's being; and it is this shift that led to other fateful changes to produce the modern problematic. All this happened because the balance between the three universals was disrupted.

There are two polar modes of viewing the self. Self-consciousness evokes, in certain circumstances, an egocentric perspective. In other circumstances, the self develops in a way that ensures its nobility. Taking note of this contrary ways of viewing the self, Jacques Maritain suggests that

'.... the human being is held between two poles: a material pole, which in reality does not concern authentic personality, but rather the material condition and the shadow, as it were, of personality; and a spiritual pole which concerns personality itself.'[lix]

Maritain, it is very clear, makes a distinction between individual and the person. Individuality, for him, is rooted in matter and is characterized by a tendency to become the centre of all things. Personality, on the other hand, inclines towards the spiritual pole and becomes the source of freedom and goodness. Man has available to him the choice of either becoming an individual or a person. Whatever he becomes, it carries certain consequences for society. As Maritain observes:

'If the development of the human being follows the direction of material individuality, he will be carried in the direction of the "hateful ego", whose law is to snatch, to absorb for oneself. In this case, personality as such will tend to adulterate, to dissolve. If, on the contrary, the development follows the direction of spiritual personality, then it will be in the direction of the generous self of the saints and heroes that man will be carried. Man will really be a person, in so far as the life of spirit and of freedom will dominate in him than of passion and of the senses'.[lx]

When the development of personality follows the direction of material individuality, then the individual will incline towards "exclusion" from one and the grassing for oneself. Man emerges as what Iris Murdoch calls a "broken totality". As a broken totality, separated from what Maritain calls "the metaphysical centre," man becomes what Plato calls "the slave of many mad masters." And these mad masters are none else but man's passions. With passion taking over the mastery of man's soul, opposition between what Rousseau calls *amour* proper (self-love) and *amour de soi* (self-concern) is inevitably introduced. This is the opposition between man's egoism, a preference for one's own interests to those of others, on the one hand, and his self-concern consisting not in a desire for self-aggrandizement but in the seeking of satisfaction for reasonable desires accompanied by benevolence, on the other.

The subject in modern times which passively reflects or responds to the reality prevailing outside is transformed into an active ego when hitched to passion. The subject that receives sense impressions passively and organizes them into knowledge mechanically, takes on a positive content as egoism when passion transforms passivity into activity. Passion is, so to speak, active passivity, responsive, reflexive action and becomes, in a sense, the essence of the self.[lxi] Active egoism becomes, in effect, the immutable essence of man, the constant factor in every stage of human development. The upgrading of self-interest as the master-passion[lxii] meant, in the one hand, a shift of focus from the world above to the lives world and, on the other, the centrality of economic activities in man's existence. In Locke's words:

'We are not born in heaven but in this world, where our being is to be preserved with meat, drink and clothing, and other necessaries that are not born with us, but must be got and kept with forecast, care and labour, and therefore, we cannot be all devotion, all praises and hallelujah, and perpetually in the vision of things above.(lxiii)

The primacy of economic activities has been justified not only on the ground of the pressing need for mobilizing material resources for survival and a comfortable living, as does Locke; it has also been justified on the ground that the satisfaction of material needs involved with production and reproduction, holds the key to the self-making of man. Karl Marx and Giambatista Vico among others are the social thinkers who argue that it is in the process of need fulfillment that man interacts with nature. In the process of interacting with nature, man realizes the potentialities that are lying dormant in the recesses of his being. As these potentialities are realized, the foundation for the development of culture is also laid; also, institutions are evolved, laws are framed, culture is cultivated, and history is made. It is also in this process that mankind moves from the stage of primitivism to civilized existence. It is true that the pursuit of self-interest becomes the ground for social discord. However, as Kant insists, without discord men might have led the life of an Arcadian shepherd in complete harmony, contentment and mutual love However, in that case, all other talents would have forever remained hidden and frozen in the stage of an embryo. As he observes:

'As gentle as the sheep they tended, such men would hardly have given for their existence a higher worth as belonged to their domesticated cattle. Thanks to be then to Nature for this unsuitableness, for this envious jealousy and vanity, for this insatiable desire for possession, or even of power! Without them all the excellent capacities implanted in mankind would slumber eternally undeveloped. Man wishes concord; but Nature knows better what is good for his species, and she will have discord.'(lxiv)

Discord may prove instrumental, as Kant insists, in the actualization of man's hidden potentialities and in overcoming the limitations of the shepherd's life; it may also be helpful in enjoying an elegant lifestyle. However, when the fulfillment of ordinary life needs concerned with the acquisition of wealth, power and prestige becomes the central quest in man's life, needs proliferate endlessly in two very significant senses. In the first place, needs become dissociated from any noble or ultimate end and become the ground of their own justification. In the second place, needs proliferate endlessly; the satisfaction of one need gives rise to other needs without any end in sight. The endlessness of needs reduces man to a part of his total being, he becomes only a tiny part of himself. He becomes only a crippled, utilitarian fragment. As a utilitarian fragment, man is reduced to nothing more than an 'externalized' creature, an object. Interest, in effect, replace(s) man's internal being and man (becomes) simply the reflexive creature of external, largely material objects which (attract) or (repel) him, his relation to those objects, of course, being to a great extent determined by his class and economic position. Man (becomes), in essence, a receptacle for interests.[(lxv)]

Man as the receptacle of interests must pit himself against others in the bitterly fought race of life even while he is forced to collaborate with others for overcoming the limitations of his insufficiency. This creates two very awkward consequences for every individual. First, once man finds himself in a situation where his individuality comes to be defined not by what he intrinsically is but by what he does or has. Devoid of any significance, except the one attributed to each individual as a producer and therefore a necessary part of the social exchange system, the individual does not exemplify anymore the dictum of Descartes, that is, 'I think, therefore, I am', but the dictum 'I possess, therefore, I am,' The individual is treated as nothing more than his role as an economic man. The interaction that takes place among individuals is not in the form of concrete individually but as abstractions. In such a society, privatization becomes an important value to be protected against social pressures. However, this poses, as Unger points out, a problem.

Alone, a man is deprived of the support of individuality. Without the social production of culture, he cannot arrive at a definition of his own identity. But in the company of others, he must conform to their expectations to be understood and to be recognized. This submission undermines his uniqueness.[(lxvi)]

Second, with interest assuming a central importance in man's life, individuals become self-defining subjects who derive their purposes from their own nature. In it they do not wish to be influenced by any authority, whether tradition, convention or social prescription, external to themselves. Self-defining subjects are essentially lonely beings radically separated from each other. In the words of de Tocqueville:

'Each of them, living apart, is a stranger to the fate of all the rest; his children and his private friends constitute to him the whole of mankind. As for the rest of his fellow citizens, he is close to them, but he does not see them; he touches them, but he does not feel them; he exists only in himself and for himself alone; and if his kindred remain with him, he may be said at any rate to have lost his country.[(lxvii)]

When individuals become self-defining subjects, society is nothing more than an aggregation of such individuals. Since society and its institutions are treated only as potential means, social relations come to be based on antagonism and reciprocal forbearance. The radically separate individuals are fated to struggle against one another, even when their antagonism must be tempered by forbearance and collaboration. While the necessity of social bonds is recognized, they are treated both as precarious and threatening to individuality. They are precarious because they are fragile in the absence of shared ends; they are threatening because greater the sharing of ends, the more the substance of individuality is likely to be eviscerated. A tension between individuality and society is thus built-in in this perspective. And, lastly, it must be emphasized that the rise of the self-defining subject is not possible without the concomitant factor of freedom and freedom today means the absence of heteronomy. However, the very supporting pillar of the individuals' self-definition, i.e., freedom, has vastly been eroded. This erosion has robbed both man as the consumer and man as a free agent. In the market mode society, the consumer is considered to be the king who makes his choices without being influenced by any authority outside of himself. However, the widespread prevalence of what is known as the 'cargo cult' has robbed him of his freedom of choice. In the marketplace, he does not get what he wants; what he gets is decided for him by producers. In so far as his agency is concerned, apart from a severe threat posed to the individual by his dedication to 'cargo cult', individual freedom itself becomes problematic. To make decisions unhampered by external constraints (that is the avoidance of heteronomy) constitutes freedom. But in making decisions,

... the individual is faced by conditions which he did not make, which are the fruits of hundreds of other wills, each of which is in a similar predicament. The way these wills concatenate is a function of blind natural law, not will. But if the point of freedom is that what I live should be decided by myself, then to the extent that I live in conditions that are only partly the fruit of my decisions, to that extent I am not integrally free.[lxviii]

Another source of threat to individual freedom lies in the emergence of vast technological, economic, political and social realms of functions, decisions, and principle of their operation. This has opened the way for the individual to fill in the empty shell of his self with contents of individuality as defined by society. In this process, what society pours into the empty shell is the need to conform, to obey and to acquiesce. As a result, the individual wishes to do what other people do (conformism) or do what he is told to do (totalitarianism). This promotes facelessness and paves the way for exploitation, domination, and consequent alienation. Even if the individual can escape the influence society exerts on him, it will not help him in making his own decisions because of two factors. The first factor is, of course, centralization, which concentrates more power of decision-making at the apex of the system than at any other echelon. As a consequence of centralization, a major portion of those decisions that vitally affected the individual's life are made not by him but by authorities at the higher echelons of the layered political system. The second factor has to do with the complexity of modern life which requires the expertise of the specialist to make highly technical decisions. This again robs the common man of his freedom.

Apart from the deleterious effect of all these factors on individual freedom and social concord, the central promise that fills individuals with hope and confidence is the promise of the good life modern times makes to all and sundry. It hangs before the expectant eyes of every deprived and depressed individual--the promissory note of plenty-- if not today, then certainly tomorrow. However, that tomorrow ever eludes. Even if modern economy succeeds in taking care of the subsistence needs of all, it can never hope to overcome the problems associated with relative deprivation that growing affluence engenders. Growing affluence neither increases wellbeing nor does it demolish the gap that exists between the affluent and those who are not so affluent. Hirsch observes:

'... Increase in resources (and thereby in the availability of goods) does nothing to increase welfare since wants increase correspondingly. The extent to which existing demands are satisfied may never increase because wants rise commensurately with resources. So, economic advancement appears as one of those hoax races that leave the participants in the same place.[lxix]

And yet there is a widespread belief that the modern industrial estate is capable of coping with the increasing wants. However, what happens is that wants themselves change and change in qualitative ways into increasingly elevated planes. Such wants tend to grow as general standards rise and with it, expectations grow that what the wealthy have today, can also be had by the rest of the population tomorrow. However, such expectations cannot be fulfilled because

The dynamic interaction between material and positional sectors becomes malign. Instead of alleviating the unmet demands of the economic system, material growth at this point exacerbates them. The locus of instability is the divergence between what is possible for the individual and what is possible for all individuals. Increased material resources enlarge the demand for positional goods, a demand that can be satisfied for some only by frustrating the demand by others. The intensified positional competition involves an increase in needs for the individual, in the sense that additional resources are required to achieve a given level of welfare; in the positional sector, individuals chase each other's tail. The race gets longer for the same prize.[lxx]

It is therefore not surprising that Mahatma Gandhi condemns modern economics as the economics of dead matter and its celebration of bodily comfort and its denigration of morality and spirituality. As he says:

An economics that inculcates Mammon Worship and enables the strong to amass wealth at the expense of the weak is a false and dismal science. It spells death. True economics, on the other hand stands for social justice, it promotes the good of all equally including the weakest, and is indispensable for a decent life.[lxxi]

The fact, however, remains that lust for life erodes internal control and renders external control ineffective; as a result, *pleonexia* assumes the character of a disease that pervades society quickly and makes the world what Sennet calls 'a peculiar mirror of the self'.

It exists to fulfill the self, there are no "human objects", object relations with a reality of their own. The peculiarity and the destructiveness of the narcissistic vision is that the more the environment of the human being is judged in terms of its convergence with or subservience to self-needs, the less fulfilling it becomes. Expectations of the outside grow enormous; the outside becomes a sea in which the self floats without differentiation. For the very reason that expectation of fulfillment becomes at once so vast and amorphous, the possibilities of fulfillment are diminished.[(lxxii)]

Even when the expectations grow and the possibility of fulfillment attenuates, efforts to acquire more and more wealth and property do not however, slacken. The narcissistic self that Sennet talks of, acquires for itself without bothering to think about the consequences of its efforts. As a result, the tendency inherent in what Mahatma Gandhi calls satanic civilization of "the strong to amass wealth at the expense of the weak," becomes all the more strong. This state of affairs has brought into being a permanently hovering of what Max Scheler calls resentment, a widespread resentment against others, especially the centralized political authority, as a result of the failure on the part of the individual to obtain those good things that make a man's life comfortable. Failing in the effort to get what one wants, people tend to blame others for their own incapacity. It is resentment in this sense that is symptomatic of the alienation that has taken a strong hold of man's world, both personal and social. It does not need to be pointed out that the root of alienation lies in the destruction of the universality of truth with the ascendance of religious dogmas since the 16 the century. Since then, a series of dogmas, roughly three, that have been identified particularly in the Comtean philosophy of history, beginning with theological dogma followed by two other dogmas -- metaphysical and ideological dogma. Since the16th century, there has been an uninterrupted reign of what Voegelin calls *dogmatomachies*.[(lxxiii)]

The world seems to be getting out of one dogma and falling into another without any end in sight.

The uninterrupted reign of *dogmatomachies* has induced a widespread belief that what comes next in the movement of time must be, or ought to be, better than what the present entails. This pervasive atmosphere of expectation fills man with hope; however, whatever time brings in the wake of its movement does not square up with what one expects. Thus, when man's expectations become apocalyptic, the world as it is constituted, proves to be a spoilsport. This has all the more deepened the sense of alienation evidenced by the alternation of man today between two disquieting states consequent upon his burning with apocalyptic fire. He is torn between being frightened by the world and full of expectations that something better will come. This brings to mind Uriah Heep, a character Charles Dickens created in *David Copperfield*, who, whenever faced by some hard times always pinned his hope on the belief that 'something will turn up'. However, that something 'better' never turns up. Moreover, alienation in modern times has been reinforced by the Enlightenment philosophy which transformed *homo credens* into *homo ludens* or *homo economicus*, who treats society and nature as the potential means of the realization of his self-determined purposes. As such, society is there to make the freedom of the self-defining subject, freedom that has emanated from human subjectivity, a real thing. This has resulted in the loss of unity, unity that bound man, society and nature together. This loss of unity manifests in a three-way split: split in the interior of man, split between man and society, and split between man and nature. As a result of these splits, the flow of life, the vital force that flows through nature, has come to be disrupted.

In so far as man himself in concerned, he now suffers from the opposition between reason and sensibility, soul and body, and reason and feeling. The rational man who is embedded in the idea of *homo economicus* must suppress all his feelings and his sentiments with a view to contemplating rationally on the means that, if adopted, can best promote his self-selected purposes. By installing the rational man seeking to protect and promote his self-interest, the Enlightenment view also installed science as the most appropriate tool of analysis of man and society. Along with it, it also celebrated a personal ethos focusing on the necessity of advancing self-interest. Enlightenment viewed man as the subject of egoistic desires, for which nature and society provided merely the means of fulfillment. It projected a philosophy that is 'utilitarian in ethical outlook, atomistic in its social philosophy, analytic in its science of man, and which (looks) to a scientific social engineering to recognize man and society and bring men happiness through perfect mutual adjustment'.[lxxiv] It is this philosophy again that has deepened the roots of alienation.

It is true that this view of man and his world has triumphed and in its triumphant march onward, it has further queered the pitch of human destiny which has been beclouded by deep crisis. However, this view has not triumphed without challenge and efforts to correct the fault-lines that had developed in the world. Three such efforts need our attention simply for the reason that they claimed to deal effectively with the emergent problems of human existence but proved inefficacious although they were associated with prestigious men and movements. These efforts are: Romanticism (or, expressivism, as Charles Taylor calls it), Kantian formulation of reconciliation between freedom and expressive unity, and Hegel who sought imaginatively to seek reconciliation between rationality, expressivism and freedom. The first reaction was expressed through a movement called Romanticism initiated by Herder, who condemned rationality as the butcher of expressivist unity of man with society and nature. Romanticism viewed science as not only cutting into the unity of human life, but also isolating the individual from society, cutting him off from nature as well; this destroyed expressive unity of man. The express intention of the Expressivist movement (Romanticism) was to restore this unity so that man could attain the highest peaks of fulfillment. In this perspective, men are expressive beings by virtue of belonging to a culture; and culture is sustained and handed down in community. The community itself on its own level is an expressive unity.[lxxv] To treat society as an instrument is, therefore, a travesty and a distortion. On the contrary, the volk, as Herder describes it, is the bearer of certain culture that sustains its members. If they isolate themselves from their cultural roots, they are certainly to be greatly impoverished. Moreover, each people had its own peculiar guiding theme or manner of expression, unique to it; it is irreplaceable and should never be suppressed; nor can it be replaced by any attempt to ape the manners of others.

This is one stream of thinking seeking to correct the errors of Enlightenment view of man and his world in the late 18th century. Concurrently, there was another stream represented by Immanuel Kant, who objected to the Enlightenment view on the ground that it objectified man along with society and nature. As an objectified entity, man's motivation also came to be caused. This was, however, unacceptable to Kant. He therefore argued that moral freedom must mean being able to decide against all inclination for the sake of the morally right. In positing this idea Kant rejected the utilitarian view of happiness by arguing that even the motivation of happiness and therefore desires cannot determine freedom. To be so determined means dispersal of man throughout his diverse desires and inclinations. Therefore, 'the morally free subject must be able to gather himself together and make a decision about his total commitment';[lxxvi] He must impose upon himself a categorical imperative which must be binding a priori. It is this categorical imperative that ensures self-determination. As such, moral life is equivalent to freedom in the sense of self-determination.

If moral freedom means autarchy, it can be then exercised only by suppressing desires and inclination. Thus, the Kantian idea of freedom extracts a heavy price; it introduces an opposition between reason and inclination and this opposition destroys peace of mind. Thus, radical freedom can be had only by suppressing desires or inclination. Moreover, autonomy, in the Kantian perspective, signifies radical freedom. This means a complete lack of heteronomy with reference to individual decision-making as well as extreme isolation of individuals from each other. Needless to say, , such a perspective leads naturally to social disorder apart from inducing disorder in man's interior. It is in this sense that Kantian solution to the Enlightenment errors does not offer any real solution. The splits remain intact. It is this situation that lends Hegelian effort aimed at reconciling the opposition between rationality, expressivism and freedom special significance; it is therefore, worth examining. The point for departure for Hegel is the spiritual principle that he posits as underlying nature; this spiritual principle is inherent in what he calls 'cosmic subjectivity'. The cosmos is pervaded by this subjectivity and man represents a microcosmic entity that reflects the whole. The spirit, or the Geist, expresses itself in the external reality of nature as well as it comes to conscious expression in man. This means that the world spirit, the Geist, completes itself with the help of self-expression through the development of self-consciousness reflected in the development of self-consciousness in man. But this occurs gradually in the movement of historical time through a dialectical process in which dualities appear and then merge to yield another higher stage, another reality.

Embedded in this view is Hegel's philosophy of history and politics. Hegel insists that all viable societies must be meaningfully articulated. This articulation is possible in a society in which energy in individual member is actively attuned to the ethos of the whole community and reflects this ethos actively in his orientation and behaviour. Hegel characterizes such a community as a moral community, a *Sittlichkeit.* This raises the issue of the voluntary cohesion of modern societies. How can free societies, societies whose institutions can function only on the basis of widespread voluntary participation, maintain their unity and their vitality? It is in answer to this very relevant question that Hegel conceives of what he calls *Sittlichkeit* (moral society). If refers to that dimension of man's ethical obligations which are to a larger life which we must sustain and continue. 'The *sittlich* dimension is important in men's ethical life where they have a profound identification with their society and its institutions'.[lxxvii] If this does not happen, alienation results. Thus, Hegel firmly believes that a free society cannot be sustained without this kind of identification which sustains a vital *sittlichkeit.* And the modern age is witness to it. Whatever philosophical criticism one can bring to bear upon the Hegelian effort at reconciliation among rationality, expressive unity and freedom, one thing is very certain, his solution has completely failed since it has not succeeded in proving its relevance or in coming into being.

The reason for this is not far to seek. One of the oblivious factors is, of course, the unchecked advance of utilitarianism which has overrun most vestiges of traditional values and institutions.

These values and institutions, needless to say, were efficacious in safeguarding people's identification with their primary groups and local communities without preventing them to develop attachments to larger groupings, such as, the state or nation. These traditional institutions have largely been destroyed by modern industrial mode of production and exchange. However, they still retain a strong hold on the people's mind. It is true that a new basis of man's identity replacing the earlier one refers to the identity of man as producer; that is, man is a being who is capable of transforming society and nature with a view to realizing his ends. He is also seen as engaging himself more and more in far-reaching transformation of society and nature. To the extent that men saw themselves this way as producers engaged in the mastering of society and nature, they tended to see society as a great collaborative enterprise in which human power becomes multiplied many times over through the combination of technology and social collaboration.[lxxviii] This has made it easy for man to prove his powers in manipulating, transforming, and controlling nature. In forcing it to yield its riches, it has also added to his hubris and confirmed himself in his rebellion against God. On the other hand, as power of manipulation/transformation had increased, he has become rootless, losing his anchor in a particular social space. In growing powerful, man has himself been transformed from somebody to nobody.

Two very fateful consequences for man and his world have followed out of these developments. In the first place, the transformation of the traditional well-knit social order into a market society has meant that continuous growth of the economy has become absolutely necessary for the appeasement of the progressively increasing hunger for goods and services to maintain as well as continuously raise the level of material well-being. The emphasis on ever-escalating growth process has engendered a set of continually rising expectations whose very endlessness ensures that they will at some point encounter frustration and hence increase, as a consequence, social tension and strain on the disciplines of society. This could provoke a crisis and uncertainty around the basic identity"[lxxix] of men as producers. This crisis of uncertainty is likely to add to the fear of the world, on the one hand, and to provoke a cycle of what Heilbroner calls 'bust and boom' in the industrial mode of production, on the other.

Second, as the pace of the industrial mode of production increases, local communities are denuded of their manpower, people tend to move out to urban centers, and as the umbilical cord of the people binding them to their culture and social status gets snapped, the process of homogenization takes longer strides. The erosion of identity and its supportive structures embedded in the traditional social order and its institutions, when coupled with the growing unrest on the economic frontier, has stimulated the appearance of radical movements with millennium hopes of laying the foundation of a new future. In the process, the belief in a new beginning for arriving at a respectful future has taken deeper roots. However, the new beginnings fail to make any dent in the structure of harsh reality. This structure has developed as a result of the dangling before every eye a promissory note of a better future; however, the very structure that keeps alive the hope of the encashment of the promissory note also frustrates this hope. As a result, unrest bred by frustrated hopes and aspirations hangs over society as a threatening cloud ready to burst into a deluge capable of sweeping the social order away. As alienation increases, unrest too spread widely and, as a consequence, traditional referents of identity formation, such as ethnicity, language, religion, etc., which have not completely been swept away by the unchecked march of modernization get politicized.

With the quickening of the process of the politicization of traditional referents of identity formation, minority alienation becomes quite acute. This boosts the mobilization of political articulation of the minority groups. Frustration in making any headway in the political arena paves the way for ethnicization of political system no rest. Homogenization thus increases minority alienation. This is because 'modern societies have moved towards much greater homogeneity and greater interdependence, so that partial communities lose their autonomy and to some extent their identity. But great differences remain; only because of the ideology of homogeneity, these differential characteristics no longer have meaning and value for those who have them.[lxxx] It is this context that we can appreciate the fact that homogenization increases minority alienation and resentment.

To remove minority alienation, two measures are usually adopted; however, their combined effect is to intensify alienation. One of these measures is, of course, the introduction of more and more doses of homogenization; but they further add to minority alienation. The other method that is usually employed is to overcome alienation by creating a society in which everyone, included the present 'but' groups, participates fully in decision-making process. This also simply aggravates the problem. The growing alienation has eroded the traditional source of allegiance, which has made consensus harder to achieve. 'As the traditional limits fade with the grounds for accepting them, society tends to fragment, partial groups become increasingly truculent in their demands as they see less reason to compromise with the system'.(lxxxi) Participation becomes effective only where there exists a prior consensus. In a situation where consensus does not obtain, participation only adds to minority alienation.

The cumulative impact of the combination of all these factors has been to deepen modern problematic. Apocalyptic hopes fail to be realized. Frustration born of alienation mounts; unrest increases, and the belief in human power to handle the emergent problem confronting modern societies erodes. This situation, needless to say, has been brought about by the liberal view of man and his world which underscores the central importance of life against the claim of good life. It is against this background that we can appreciate the message contained in the Urdu couplet; *Maut hai ek lafze bemani; Jisko mara hayat ne mara* (Death is a meaningless term; whoever dies is killed by the lust for life). Efforts to seek solution to this problematic, we have seen, do not or cannot prove efficacious. It is in this context of the perception of widespread befuddlement and confusion that forcefully draws our attention to the solution of the contemporary problematic in the wisdom of the past. It is a travesty to think that the three perspectives of the past delineated represent a cosmic view of the world to which one must turn one's back in order to live a good life. It is true that all of them insist on turning one's back as is reflected in such terms as the Greek *periagoge*, the Buddhist *paravritti* and the Vedic *pratiyantam*. However, what they mean is to overcome the lust of the body with a view to achieving self-control. It is self-control that restricts hubris as a means of achieving sophrosyne, that is, learning to know the limits of human power and ambition.

All the three perspectives from the past that we have discussed above underline the need for subjugating the pursuit of material goals under the suzerainty and guidance of certain spiritual values. Additionally, they also call for creating a social system that is compatible with and supportive of the developmental needs of man. What should also be emphasized here is the fact that the call to return to the past wisdom for overcoming modern problematic signifies only deriving certain insights from it, not to imitate it. The past as it was articulated in its institutional mode is dead and gone. What is left of it is only certain insights that help us to understand our predicament and suggest ways of getting out of it. To accept these insights is not to revive the past, but to derive from it certain insights which can help us in using certain clues for reconstructing a social order compatible with man's spiritual needs. By going to the past, we do not seek to restore it but only to open the horizon of the future where man can have peace and harmony.

References

1. Brahmananda P.R. 1971. "A Theoretical note on the Economic Foundation of a *Gandhi type society" in Raval M.N. et. al. (Eds), Gandhiji's Economic Thought and its Relevance at Present,* South Gujrat University, Surat.
2. Dasgupta Ajit K. 1996. *Gandhi's Economic Thought,* Routledge, London.
3. Desai Meghnad, 1988. "Development Perspective: Was there an Alternative to Mahalanobis", in Ahluwalia Isher Judge, Little I.M.D. (Eds.). 1998. *India's Economic Reforms and Development Essays,* Oxford University Press, Delhi.
4. Diwan Romesh and Lutz Mark (editors) 1985. Essays in Gandhian Economics, Gandhi Peace Foundation, New Delhi.
5. Gandhi Rajmohan 1956. *The Good Boatman: A Portrait of Gandhi,* Penguin Books, New Delhi.
6. Government of India 2000. *Collected Works of Mahatma Gandhi,* Volume 15, 4th revised edn, Publications Division, Ministry of Information and Broadcasting, Gol, New Delhi.
7. Gullien Mauro F. 2001. "Is Globalisation Civilising Destructive or Feeble? A Critique of Five Key Database in the Social Science Literature", in *Annual Review of Sociology,* Vol. 27, 2001 Wharton School and Department of Sociology, University of Pennsylvania, USA.

8. Hanley Nik, Shogren Jason F. and White Ben 1997. *Environmental Economics in Theory and Practice*, Macmillan, Delhi.
9. Hug A.M. 1985. "The Doctrine of Internal Trade: A Gandhian Perspective". in Diwan Romesh and Lutz Mark (Eds), 1985, *Essays in Gandhian Economics*, Gandhi Peace Foundation, New Delhi.
10. Iyenger Sudershan 2005. "Sustainable Development and Indian Economy: Some Reflections", E.F. Schumacher Memorial Lecture delivered at the Nagpur University on February 5, 2005.
11. Lakdawal D.T. 1971. "Gandhiji and Growth Economic", in Raval M.N. et. al. (Eds.), *Gandhiji's Economic Thought and its Relevance at Present*, South Gujrat University, Surat.
12. Parel Anthony J. (Editor) 1997. *Gandhi: Hind Swaraj and Other Writings*, Foundation Books, New Delhi for Cambridge University Press, U.K.
13. Raval M.N. 1971. "Contentment and Containment of Wants - A Suggested Interpretation", in Raval M.N. et al. (Eds), *Gandhiji's Economic Thought and its Relevance at Present*, South Gujrat University, Surat.
14. Sethi J. D. 1978. *Gandhi Today*, Vikas Publishing House Pvt. Ltd., New Delhi.
15. Siddharthan N.S. 1985. *The Gandhian Thought and the Information (Fourth Industrial) Revolution*', Indian Economic Association, Conference Volume, 68th Annual Conference, Ahmedabad

NOTES

(i) For those who are interested in the full reference is: Donnella Meadows and others 1972. The limits to Growth: A report for the club of Rome's Project on the Predicament of Mankind. A Potomac Associates book, Pan Book London and Sydney.

(ii) I have elsewhere reviewed the debate on sustainable development and tried to show the link between the present day concerns shown by the environmental movement and the concerns expressed by Gandhiji. See Iyangar 2005.

(iii) Professor Jevons became the President of the Indian Economic Association's 5th Annual Conference held in Patna during March 1922.

(iv) See The Rigveda VIII, 58.2.

(v) Yajurveda, 31.9.

(vi) Isopnishad, I. The mantra reads: Ishavasyaidam sarvam, yatkinchit jagatyam jagat...

(vii) For a discussion on this, See Ramashray Roy, Beyond Ego's Domain, Being and order in the Veda (Delhi, Shipra Publications, 1989) pp. 117-18.

(viii) It must be pointed out that this understanding of psyche is quite different either from the Homeric or from modern understanding. The term psyche in Homer means the life force in the physical sense, which leaves a man when he dies, for instance, the blood. However, when we come to Pythagoras, we notice a transformation of the meaning of the term psyche as has been pointed out. What is also important to note in this connection is that beginning with the seventeenth century the term psyche was replaced by another term, that is, consciousness. In its modern guise, psyche or consciousness does not signify anything more than a storehouse of information about the individual himself and his relationship with the outer world.

(ix) Needless to say, that this formulation does not conform to the Aristotelian conceptualization of the relationship between form and matter.

(x) Voegelin, "The Drama of Humanity", in *Drama of Humanity and Miscellaneous Essays*, p. 186.

(xi) Cf. Hannah Arendt, *The Human Condition* (Garden City, New York, Anchor Books, 1959).

(xii) S. Dasgupta, *A History of Indian Philosophy*, 5 vols. (London: Cambridge University Press, 1965), II, p. 453.

(xiii) Heracitus, quoted in Werner Jaeger, *Paideia* (New York: Oxford University Press, 1939), I, p. 180.

(xiv) This is what Taittriya Brahman 2.8.1 underlines when it observes that the preservation of the cosmic order depends on ensuring the continuity of the process of exchange between man, gods and other beings. It is the process of exchange that maintains the cosmic metabolism.

(xv) The terms in the system refer to beings with different levels of consciousness. Adhyataman refers to the Supreme Spirit manifest as the self of the individual, while adhidaivam signifies the consciousness that we ascribe to superior beings such as Gods. In contrast to both, adhibhautik refers to the Supreme Spirit operating in material objects.

(xvi) He ascribed hypocrisy to modern civilization when he came across in 1910 a cartoon published in an English journal, *The New Age*. He describes the cartoon thus:

It shows an army on the march. Behind, there is a grotesque figure, that of a general. On the body of this terrible form is hanging a gun, emitting smoke in every direction, and swords dripping with blood, and on its head a cannon. There is the drawing of a skull on a bande hanging on one side. On the arm moreover there is a cross (this the emblem of a badge which looks after the wounded), in the mouth held in the teeth, there is a dagger dripping with blood. On the shoulder is seen a belt studded with live cartridges.

Mahatma Gandhi considers this cartoon as symptomatic of modern civilization, although it is directly related to the brutality of the ways of modern times.

(xvii) *Collected Works of Mahatma Gandhi*, 100 Vol. (Delhi: The Publications Division, Ministry of Information and Broadcasting, Government of India, 1959), Vol. X, p. 202 (Emphasis added).

(xviii) *Republic* 368 E 2-3.

(xix) Ibid., 372d 4-5.

(xx) Darrell Dobbs, "Choosing Justice. Socrates" Model City and the Practice of Dialectic". *American Political Science Review*, 88, 2 (June 1994), p. 206.

(xxi) *The Republic of Plato*, tr. F. M. Comford (New York: Oxford University Press, 1965), p. 61.

(xxii) Loc. cit.

(xxiii) Ibid.

(xxiv) Dobbs, op. cit., p. 267.

(xxv) *Republic*, 373b, 3-4.

(xxvi) Plato, Phaedo, 81B.

(xxvii) Ibid, Jowett edition, III, p. 197.

(xxviii) *Republic*, 3290C.

(xxix) Ibid., 527 A-E.

(xxx) Ibid., 533D.

(xxxi) On this point, see Jaeger, op. cit., p. 48.

(xxxii) *Republic*, 540-a-b.

(xxxiii) Jaeger, op. cit., p. 39.

(xxxiv) On this point see, Eric Voegelin, Plato (Baton Rouge: Louisiana State University Press, 1966), pp. 112-16.

(xxxv) Jaeger, op. cit., p. 45.

(xxxvi) Nichomachean Ethics (NE), 1095b 14ff.

(xxxvii) Ibid., 1103 a5-10.

(xxxviii) Ibid., 1129b9.

(xxxix) *Politics*, 12789b, 15-25 (Barker's translation)

(xl) Charles Taylor "Growth Legitimacy and the Modern Identity". Praxis International, 1,2 (July 1981), p. 112.

(xli) John M. Cooper, *Reason and Human Good in Aristotle* (Cambridge University Press, 1975, p. 83).

(xlii) *Politics*, 1257b - C9

(xliii) Ibid., 1258a 17.

(xliv) Ibid., 1258a 16.

(xlv) Ibid., 1258a 17.

(xlvi) For the discussion of the symbolic meaning of *Vritra*, see Ramashray Roy, *Beyond Ego's Domain: Being and Order in the Veda* (Delhi: Shipra Publications, 1999), p. 194, fn. 42.

(xlvii) Atharvaveda, XI, 8.18 and 30.

(xlviii) Briharanyak Upanishad, II.I.20, Mundak Upnanishad II.I.I

(xlix) The Vedic thinking attributes this lack of harmony to *avidya* (nescience). Avidya, as Abhinava Gupta says, is twofold, the innate (purusha) the auto-limitation of God - the consequence of his voluntary decline in time and a space - and intellective ignorance (buddhigata) increased by ourselves. See his Tantrasara, p. 3. Quoted in Guiseppe T. Gucci, *The Theory and Practice of the Mandalas* (London: Rider & Co., 1974), p. 47.

(l) The Universal Self conceived in the Vedic philosophy as having five essences, such as eternity (*nityatwa*), all prevailing (*vyapakahwa*), plenitude (*purnatwa*), omniscience (*sarvagnata*), and omnipotence (*sarva kartritva*). See Tattiriya Upanishad, II.II.

(li) Tucci, op. cit., p. 10.

(lii) Rigveda, I. 164.20.

(liii) Atharvaveda, X, 8.32.

(liv) Chhandagya Upanishad, 8. 1201.

(lv) Cf. Kathopanishad I. 11.6 which underlines that "the means for the attainment of the other world does not become revealed to the non-discriminating man who blunders being befooled by the lure of wealth. One who constantly thinks that there is only this world and none hereafter, comesunder my (Death's) sway again and again.

(lvi) Ananda C. Coomarswamy, "Windows of the Soul" in *What is Civilization?* (Delhi: Oxford University Press, 1989), p. 53.

(lvii) MandukyaUpanishad, III.II.2.

(lviii) Taittiriya Brahmana, 2.8.1.

(lix) Jacques Maritain, *Challenges and Renewals: Selected Readings*, eds. Joseph W. Evans and Leo R. Ward (Notre Dame: University of Notre Dame Press 1966), p. 265.

(lx) Ibid., pp. 290-91.

(lxi) John Locke, *An Essay Concerning Human Understanding*, pr. K.OO, Chapter XXVII, article 11.

(lxii) On this, see Albert Hirschman, *Passions and Interests: Political Arguments for Capitalism before its Triumph* (Princeton: Princeton University Press, 1977), pp. 31-66.

(lxiii) Quoted in Sheldon S. Wolin, *Politics and Vision* (Boston: Little Brown & Co. Inc. 1960), p. 298.

(lxiv) Immanuel Kant, *Principles of Politics*, Quoted in Lucio Colleti; *From Rousseau to Lenin: Studies in Ideology and Society*, trans. John Merrington and Judith While (New York: Monthly Review Press, 1972), pp. 159-60.

(lxv) Ellen M. Wood, *Mind and Politics: An Approach to the Meaning of Liberal and Socialist Individualism* (Berkeley: University of California Press, 1972), p. 111.

(lxvi) Roberto M. Unger, *Knowledge and Politics* (New York: Free Press, 1975), pp. 156-57.

(lxvii) Alexis de Tocqueville, *Democracy in America* (2 Vols.), ed. Phillips Bradley (New York: Vintage Books, 1956), II, p. 336.

(lxviii) Charles Taylor, *Hegel and Modern Society* (Cambridge, Cambridge University Press, 1979), p. 106.

(lxix) Fred Hirsch, *Social Limits to Growth* (London: Routledge & Kegan Paul, 1977), p. 60.

(lxx) Ibid., p. 67.

(lxxi) Mahatma Gandhi, *Sarvodaya*, ed. Bharatan Kumarappa (Ahmedabad: Navjivan Publishing House, 1954), p. 33.

(lxxii) Rechard Sennet, "Destructive Gemeinschaft", in Norman Bimbaum, ed. *Beyond the Crisis* (London: Oxford University Press, 1977), pp. 177.

(lxxiii) Eric Voegetin, "The Drama of Humanity", in *Drama of Humanity and Miscellaneous Essays* (Missouri: University of Missouri Press, 2001), p. 195.

(lxxiv) Charles Taylor, Hegel and Modern Society (Cambridge: Cambridge University Press, 1979), p. 10.

(lxxv) Ibid., p. 2.

(lxxvi) Ibid., p. 3.

(lxxvii) Ibid., p. 125.

(lxxviii) Ibid., p.128.

(lxxix) Ibid., p. 129.

(lxxx) Ibid., p. 114.

(lxxxi) Ibid., p. 115.

Bibliography

Adams, Nassau A. (1993). *Worlds Apart, The North-South Divide and the International System*, London and New Jersey, Zed Books.

Agathangelou, Anna M. (2004). 'Power, Borders, Security, Wealth: Lessons of Violence and Desire from September 11', *International Studies Quarterly*, Vol. 48.

Alejandro, Carlos Diaz (1981). 'The Less Developed Countries and Transnational Enterprises', Grassman, Sven and Lundberg, Eric (eds.), *The World Economic Order, Past and Prospects*, London, Macmillan.

Algieri, Franco (2002). 'EU Economic Relations with China: An Institutional Perspective', *The China Quarterly*, No. 169, March.

Amiya Kumar Bagchi (1998). 'Growth Miracle and Its Unraveling in East and South East Asia', *Economic and Political Weekly*, 33(18), May 2-8.

Anderson, Ben, (2002). 'Long Live the Nation', *Biblio*, Special Issue.

Annel, L. and Nygren, B. (1980). *The Developing Countries and the World Economic Order*, London, Methuen.

Aseniero, Gorge (1996). 'Asia in the World System', Chew, Sing C. and Denemark, Robert A. (ed.), *The Underdevelopment of Development*, New Delhi, Sage Publications.

Asian Development Bank, 1995, 1998, 2000, *Asian Development Outlook*, New York, Oxford University Press.

Baldwin, (1987). 'Power Analysis and World Politics; New Trends versus Old Tendencies', in Knorr, Klaus (ed.), *Power, Strategy, and Security*, New Delhi, Asian Books.

Ballance, R.H., J.A. Ansari, Singer, H.W. (1982). *The International Economy and Industrial Development: The Impact of Trade and Investment on the Third World*, UK, Wheatsheaf Books Ltd.

Barkawi, T. and Laffey, M. (2006). 'The Imperial Peace: Democracy, Force and Globalization', James, P. and Friedman, J. (eds), *Globalization and Violence*, Vol. 1, London, Sage Publications.

Bayne, Nicholas (2002). 'The G8 Summit and Global Governance: The Message of Okinawa', Kirton, John J. and Takase, J. (eds), *New Directions in Global Political Governance,* England, Ashgate.

Beedham, Brian (1999). 'The New Geopolitics', *The Economist,* 31 July-6 August, London.

Beeson, Mark (2003). 'Sovereignty under Siege: Globalization and the State in Southeast Asia', *Third World Quarterly,* 24(2).

Bernstein, H. 1981, *Underdevelopment and Development,* England, Penguin Books.

Bhaduri, Amit (2002). 'Nationalism and Economic Policy in the Era of Globalization', Nayyar, Deepak (ed.), *Governing Globalization, Issues and Institutions,* New Delhi, Oxford Univ. Press.

Bhagwati, Jagdish (2004). *In Defense of Globalization,* New Delhi, Oxford Univ. Press.

Boltho, Andrea (2001). 'Reconstruction after Two World Wars - Why the Differences?' *The Journal of European Economic History,* 30(2).

Brandt, Willy et al, (1980). *North South: A Programme for Survival,* (The Report of the Independent Commission on International Development issues under the Chairmanship of Willy Brandt), London, Pan Books.

Brenner, Robert (1998). 'The Economics of Global Turbulence', *New Left Review,* No. 229, May/June.

Brown, Lester R. (1973). *World without Borders,* New Delhi, Affiliated East-West Press Pvt. Ltd.

Bruhl, Tanja and Rittberger, Volker (2001). 'From international to global governance: Actors, collective decision-making, and the United Nations in the world of the twenty-first century', Rittberger, Volker (ed.), *Global Governance and the United Nations System,* Tokyo, United Nations Univ. Press.

Bullard, Nicola, et al, (1998). 'Taming the Tigers: The IMF and the Asian Crisis', Jomo, K.S. (ed.), *Tigers in Trouble, Financial Governance, Liberalization and Crises in East Asia,* London and New York, Zed Books Ltd.

Burbach, R., Nunez, O., Kagarlitsky, B. (1997). '*Globalization and its Discontents*', London, Pluto Press.

Castro, Fidel (1984). *The World Crisis, Its Economic and Social Impact on the Underdeveloped Countries,* London, Zed Books Ltd.

Chatterjee, Partha (2004). *The Politics of the Governed,* Delhi, Permanent Black.

Chaudhury, P.K., Kelkar, V.L. and Vikash. Y. (2004). 'The Evolution of "Homegrown Conditionality" in India: IMF Relations', *Journal of Development Studies,* 40(6), August.

Chomsky, Noam (1993). *Year 501, The Conquest Continues*, London, Verso.
Chomsky, Noam (1996). *'World Orders, Old and New'*, lecture delivered at Jawaharlal Nehru University (New Delhi), January.
Cohen, Jean L. (2008). 'Whose Sovereignty? Empire versus International Law', in Cameron, Angus et al (ed.), *International Political Economy*, Vol. V, London, Sage Publications.
Cole, G.D.H., (1947). *The Intelligent Man's Guide to the Post-War World*, London, Victor Gollanez Ltd.
Cole, J.P. (1979). *Geography of World Affairs*, England, Penguin Books.
Colijn, Ko. (2004)., 'Weapons of Mass Destruction, A Medium Power Concern'?, *International Journal*, Vol. LIX, No. 2, Spring.
Commission of the European Communities, 2001, White Paper.
Commission on Global Governance (1995). *'Our Global Neighbourhood'*, New York, Oxford University Press.
Cooper, Andrew F. (2002). 'Like-minded nations, NGOs, and the changing pattern of diplomacy within the UN system: An Introductory Perspective', Cooper, Andrew F. et al (ed.), *Enhancing Global Governance*, Delhi, Bookwell.
Cox, Robert W. (2008). 'Social Forces, States and World Orders: Beyond International Relations Theory', Cameron, Angus et al (ed.), *International Political Economy*, Vol. I, London, Sage Publications.
Dandekar, C. (1990). *Surveillance, Power and Modernity*, Policy Press.
Darwin, John, (1988). *Britain and Decolonization, The Retreat from Empire in the Post-War World*, London, Macmillan.
Datta Chaudhuri, M.K. (1981). 'Industrialization and Foreign Trade: The Development Experiences of South Korea and the Philippines', in Lee, Eddy (ed.), *Export-led Industrialization and Development*, Geneva, ILO.
Dogra, Bharat (2003). 'Continuing Invasion', *Frontier*, June 1-7.
Dunning, John H. (1990). 'Changes in the Level and Structure of International Production: The Last One Hundred Years', Buckley, Peter J. (ed.), *International Investment*, England, Edward Elgar Pub. Ltd.
Eyal, Jonathan (2005). 'European Defense: Illusions Continued', in *The European Union Encyclopedia and Directory*, 2005, London and New York, Europa Publications.
Falk, Richard (2002). 'The United Nations System: Prospects for Renewal', Nayyar, Deepak (ed.), *Governing Globalization, Issues and Institutions*, New Delhi, Oxford University Press.
Farhang, Mansoir (1979). 'Imperialism: A Transnational System of Privilege', Grieves, Forest L. (ed.), *'Transnationalism in World Politics and Business'*, New York, Pergamon Press.

Faria, Carlos Ramirez (1991). *The Origins of Economic Inequality between Nations*, London, Unwin Hyman.

Frank, Andre Gunder (1998). *Reorient: Global Economy in an Asian Age*, New Delhi, Vistaar Publications.

Gamble, Andrew (1990). 'Britain's Decline: Some Theoretical Issues', Mann, Michael (ed.), *The Rise and Decline of the Nation State*, Oxford, UK, Basil Blackwell Ltd.

Gardner, Richard N. (1972). 'The Political Setting', Acheson, Keith, A.L., Chant, John H., and Prachowny, Martin F. (eds.), *Bretton Woods Revisited*, London, Macmillan.

Geddes, Andrew (2005). 'Migration and Asylum Policy', *The European Union Encyclopedia and Directory*, 2005, London and New York, Europa Publications.

Gilpin, R. (2001). Global Political Economy, London, Orient Longman.

Girling, R.H. (1985). *Multinational Institutions and the Third World*, New York, Praeger Pub.

Gomes, (2003). *The Economies and Ideology of Free Trade: A Historical Review*, Cheltenham, Edward Elgar.

Government of India, Ministry of External Affairs, 1991, *New Economic Policy*, New Delhi.

Government of India, Ministry of Finance, 1999-2005, *Economic Survey*, New Delhi.

Griffin, Keith (1981). 'Economic Development in a Changing World', *World Development*, 9(8), March.

Griffin, Keith (1996). *Studies in Globalization and Economic Transitions*, London, Macmillan Press.

Griffin, Keith (2003). 'Economic Globalization and Institutions of Global Governance', *Development and Change*, 34 (5).

Halabi, Yakub (2008). 'The Expansion of Global Governance into the Third World: Altruism, Realism, or Constructivism?', Cameron, Angus et al. (ed.), *International Political Economy*, Vol. III, London, Sage Publications.

Hall, John A. (1990). 'Will the United States Decline as did Britain?', Mann, Michael (ed.), *The Rise and Decline of the Nation State*, Basil Oxford, UK, Blackwell Ltd.

Harris, Jerry (2006). 'Dreams of Global Hegemony and the Technology of War', James, P. and Friedman, J. (ed.), *Globalization and Violence*, Vol. 1, London, Sage Publications.

Harrod, Sir Roy (1972). 'Problems Perceived in the International Financial System', Acheson, A.L. Keith, Chant, John H. and Prachowny, Martin F. (ed.), *Bretton Woods Revisited*, London, Macmillan.

Hasley, A.H. (1994). 'Sociology as a Political Arithmetic', *British Journal of Sociology*, 45(3), Sept.

Hattori, Tamio and Sato, Yukihito (1997). 'A Comparative Study of Development Mechanisms in Korea and Taiwan: Introductory Analysis', *Developing Economies*, 35(4), December.

Haynes, Michael (1998). 'European Union and its Periphery, Inclusion and Exclusion', *Economic and Political Weekly*, August 29.

Held, David and McGrew, Anthony (2008). 'The End of the Old Order? Globalization and the Prospects for World Order', Cameron, Angus et al. (ed.), *International Political Economy*, Vol. IV, London, Sage Publications.

Helleiner, Gerry (2002). 'Developing Countries in Global Economic Governance and Negotiation Processes', Nayyar, Deepak (ed.), *Governing Globalization, Issues and Institutions*, New Delhi, Oxford University Press.

Hettne, Bjorn (1990). *Development Theory and the Three Worlds*, England, Longman Scientific and Technical.

Higgot, Richard (2001). 'Economic globalization and global governance: Towards a post-Washington Consensus?', Rittberger, Volker (ed.), *Global Governance and the United Nations System*, Tokyo, United Nations Univ. Press.

Hirsch, Joachim (2008). 'Nation-State, International Regulation and the Question of Democracy', in Cameron, Angus et al. (ed.), *International Political Economy*, Vol. I, London, Sage Publications.

Hoffman, Stanley (2003). 'US-European Relations: Past and Future', *International Affairs*, Vol. 79, No.5.

Hogg, William, (2004). 'Controlling Weapons in Turbulent Times, *International Journal*, Vol. LIX, No.2, Spring.

Holland, R.F. (1985). *European Decolonization 1918-1981, An Introductory Survey*, London, Macmillan.

Hoogvelt, Ankei (1997). *Globalization and the Post-Colonial World, The New Political Economy of Development*, London, Macmillan.

Hudson, Michael (2008). Super Imperialism: The Origin and Fundamentals of US World Dominance Introduction, Cameron, Angus et al. (ed.), *International Political Economy*, Vol. V, London, Sage Publications.

Hudson, Ray (2004). 'Conceptualizing Economies and Their Geographies: Spaces, Flows and Circuits', *Progress in Human Geography*, 28(4).

Hung, Rudy (1996). 'The Great U-Turn in Taiwan: Economic Restructuring and a Surge in Inequality', *Journal of Contemporary Asia*, 26(2).

Huntington, Samuel P. (1997). *The Clash of Civilizations and the Remaking of World Order*, India, Viking, Penguin.

Hymer, Stephen (1990). 'The Multinational Corporation and the Law of Uneven Development', Bowles, Samuel and Edwards, Richard (eds), *Radical Political Economy*, Vol. II, England, Edward Elgar Publication Ltd.

IMF, 1983-2003, *World Economic Outlook*, several issues, Washington D.C., U.S.A.

IMF, *International Financial Statistics*, several issues, Washington D.C., U.S.A.

Ivision, D. (2002). *Post-Colonial Liberalism*, New York, Cambridge Univ. Press.

James, Paul (2006). 'Post-dependency? The Third World in an Era of Globalism and Late-Capitalism', James, P. and Friedman, J. (eds), *Globalization and Violence*, Vol. 1, London, Sage Publications.

Jesupatham, Samuel (2003). 'An Imperial Gesture', *Frontier*, April 20-26.

Jones, G.S. (1979). 'The History of US Imperialism', Blackburn, Robin (ed.), *Ideology in Social Science*, UK, Fontana/ Collins.

Jones, R. and Philips, R. (2006). 'Unsettling Geographical Horizons: Exploring Pre-modern and Non-European Imperialism', James, P. and Friedman, J. (eds), *Globalization and Violence*, Vol. 1, London, Sage Publications.

Kapstein, Ethan (1998). 'Trade Liberalization and the Politics of Trade Adjustment Assistance', *International Labour Review*, 137(4).

Kapur, Devesh (2002). 'Processes of Change in International Organizations', in Nayyar, Deepak (ed.), *Governing Globalization, Issues and Institutions*', New Delhi, Oxford University Press.

Karim, Mohammad, A.R.A. (1996). 'The Arab's Ideas on Shaping a New World Order and Their Concepts about U.N.O.', *Indian Journal of Politics*, 30(1&2).

Kirton, John, J., (2001). 'The G20: Representativeness, Effectiveness, and Leadership in Global Governance', Kirton, John et al. (ed.), *Guiding Global Order: G-8 Governance in the Twenty-First Century*, England, Ashgate.

Kirton, John, J. (2002). 'The G8, the United Nations, and Global Security Governance', Kirton, John J. and Takase, J. (eds.), *New Directions in Global Political Governance*, England, Ashgate.

Kirton, John, J., and Takase, J. (2002). '*New Directions in Global Political Governance*: Challenges and Responses', Kirton, John J. and Takase, J. (eds.), New Directions in Global Political Governance, England, Ashgate.

Kleinknecht A. and Wengel, J.T. (1998). 'The Myth of Economic Globalization', *Cambridge Journal of Economics*, 30(26), July 1.

Knight, W. Andy (2002). 'The Future of the UN Security Council: Questions of Legitimacy and Representation in Multilateral Governance', in Cooper, F. Andrew et al. (eds.), *Enhancing Global Governance: Towards a New Diplomacy?* Delhi, Bookwell.

Kruijer, G.J. (1987). *Development through Liberation: Third World Problems and Solutions*, London, Macmillan.

Kurosawa, Mitsuru (2002). 'Curbing Nuclear Proliferation: Japanese, G8 and Global Approaches', Kirton, John J. and Takase, J. (eds), *New Directions in Global Political Governance*, England, Ashgate.

Lagasse, Philippe, (2004). 'The International Criminal Court and the Foreign Policies of the United States', *International Journal*, Vol. LIX, Spring.

Lall, S., (2002). 'Transnational Corporations and Technology Flows', in Nayyar, Deepak (ed.), *Governing Globalization, Issues and Institutions*, New Delhi, Oxford Univ. Press.

Lee, William, K.M. (1997). 'Foreign Investment, Industrial Restructuring and Dependent Development in Singapore', *Journal of Contemporary Asia'*, 27(1).

Lyon, Peter (1980). 'ASEAN after ten years: problems and prospects for regional and functional cooperation within Southeast Asia', Matsumoto, S. (ed.), *Southeast Asia in a Changing World,* Tokyo, Japan, Institute of Developing Economies.

Maddison, Angus (1982). *Phases of Capitalist Development*, New York, Oxford University Press.

Magdoff, Harry (1969). *The Age of Imperialism, The Economics of US Foreign Policy*, New York, Modern Reader Paperback.

Majumder, Bhaskar (1997). 'Globalization of Large Economies (L-7), *Asian Economic Review,* 39(2), Aug.

Majumder, Bhaskar (1998). 'Extensive Globalization: Compulsions of Big Power and Scope for Large Economies', *Review of Development & Change*, Vol. 3, No. 1, January-June.

Majumder, Bhaskar (2000). 'Regional Integration with the European Union as a Case: Any Lessons for the Third World?', *Journal of Social and Economic Change*, 2(2), March.

Marx, K. and Engels, F. (1977). *Manifesto of the Communist Party*, Moscow, Progress Publishers.

Miliband, Ralph (1989). 'State Power and Capitalist Democracy', Bharadwaj, K. and Kaviraj, S. (eds.), *Perspectives on Capitalism*, New Delhi, Sage Publications.

Modelski, G. and Morgan, P. M. (2006). 'Understanding Global War', James, P. and Friedman, J. (eds), *Globalization and Violence*, Vol. 3, London, Sage Publications.

Moellendorf, Darrel (1994). 'Marxism, Internationalism, and the Justice of War', *Science and Society*, 58(3), Fall.

Moore, Mike, (2003). 'A World without Walls: Freedom, Development, Free Trade and Global Governance', Cambridge, UK, Cambridge University Press.

Morgan, T. Clifton and Bickers, Kenneth, N. (1992). 'Domestic Discontent and the External Use of Force', *The Journal of Conflict Resolution*, 36(1), March.

Mundell, Robert. A. (1972). 'The Future of the International Financial System', Acheson, A.L. Keith, Chant, John H. and Prachowny, Martin F. (ed.), *Bretton Woods Revisited*, London, Macmillan.

Myrdal, Gunnar (1982). *Asian Drama, An Inquiry into the Poverty of Nations*, Vol. I, New Delhi, Kalyani Publishers.

Nailor, Peter (1980). 'Military Strategy', Taylor, Trevor (ed.), *Approaches and Theory in International Relations*, London, Longman.

Nayyar, Deepak (2002a). 'Cross-border Movements of People', Nayyar, Deepak (ed.), *Governing Globalization, Issues and Institutions*, New Delhi, Oxford University Press.

Nayyar, Deepak (2002b). 'Towards Global Governance', in Nayyar, Deepak (ed.), *Governing Globalization, Issues and Institutions*, New Delhi, Oxford University Press.

Nayyar, Deepak (2002c). 'The Existing System and the Missing Institutions', Nayyar, Deepak (ed.), *Governing Globalization, Issues and Institutions*, New Delhi, Oxford University Press.

Nye, J.S. and Keohane, R.O. (2006). 'Transnational Relations and World Politics: A Conclusion', in James, P. and Friedman, J. (ed.), *Globalization and Violence*, Vol. 4, London, Sage Publications.

O 'Brien, Patrick K. (1990). 'The Imperial Component in the Decline of British Economy Before 1914 ', Mann, Michael (ed.), *The Rise and Decline of the Nation State*, Oxford, UK, Basil Blackwell Ltd.

Okuda, Satoru (1997). 'Industrialization Policies of Korea and Taiwan and their Effects on Manufacturing Productivity', *Developing Economies*, 35(4), Dec.

Oppermann, Thomas (1986). 'A New International Economic Order and International Economic Law' in *Law and State*, Vol. 33, ed. by The Institute of Scientific Cooperation, Tubingen.

Padison, (1983). *Fragmented State: The Political Geography of Power*, Oxford, London, Basil Blackwell.

Palan, Ronen et al, (2008). 'The State in the *Global Political Economy*' in Cameron, Angus, et al. (ed.), *International Political Economy*, Vol. II, London, Sage Publications.

Panitch, Leo (2000). 'The New Imperial State', *New Left Review*, March-April, No. 2.

Paris, Ronald (2006). 'Peacekeeping and the Constraints of Global Culture', in James, P. and Nairn, T. (Eds), *Globalization and Violence*, Vol. 3, London, Sage Publications.

Park, Yung, Chul (1981). 'Export-led Development: The Korean Experience 1960-78', in Lee, Eddy (ed.), *Export-led Industrialization and Development*, Geneva, Switzerland, ILO.

Paulantzas, Nicos (1968). *Political Power and Social Classes*, London, Verso.

Paulantzas, Nicos (1978). *State, Power, Socialism*, London, Verso.

Peck, J., and Yeung, H. (2003). *Remaking the Global Economy,* London, Sage Publications.

Peou, Sorpong, (2001). 'Security-community Building for Better Global Governance', in Rittberger, Volker (ed.), *Global Governance and the United Nations System*, Tokyo, United Nations Univ. Press.

Petras, James and Davenport, Christian (1995). 'Winning the Cold War and US Industrial Decline', 1960-90', *Journal of Contemporary Asia*, 25(3).

Petras, James and Morley, Morris, (1998). 'US French Relations in the New World order', *Economic and Political Weekly*, 33(16), April 18-24.

Planning Commission, GOI, Tenth Five-Year Plan, 2002-2007, New Delhi.

Rajan, M.S. (2003). 'US-UK Aggression against Iraq and the New World Order', *Mainstream*, April 12.

Rasiah, Rajah (1994). 'Capitalist Industrialization in ASEAN', *Journal of Contemporary Asia*, 24(2).

Reed, James (2002). "Why is the USA not a like-minded country? Some structural notes and historical considerations', in Cooper, Andrew F. et al. (ed.), *Enhancing global governance: Towards a New Diplomacy?*, Delhi, Bookwell.

Robertson, R. and Inglis, D. (2006). 'The Global Aminus: In the Tracks of World Consciousness', in James, P. and Nairn, T. (eds.), *Globalization and Violence*, Vol. 1, London, Sage Publications.

Rostow, W. W. (1960). *The Stages of Economic Growth*, London, Cambridge Univ. Press.

Roy, A.K. (2003). 'Meaning of America's Iraq War', *Frontier*, April 27-May 3.

Sauvant, Karl P. (1981). Sauvant Karl P. (ed.), *Changing Priorities on the International Agenda, The New International Economic Order*, Oxford, England, Pergamon Press.

Schonberg, K. Karl (2004). 'Global Security and Legal Restraint; Reconsidering War Powers after Sept. 11', *Political Science Quarterly*, 119(1).

Scott, Andrew G. (2005). 'Economic Integration in the European Union', in *The European Union Enclopedia and Directory*, 2005, London and New York, Europa Publications.

Sen, Amartya (2004). 'Social Exclusion, Concept, Applications, Scrutiny', *Critical Quest*, New Delhi, India.

Smith, Michael (2005). 'The External Relations of the European Union', in The European Union Enclopedia and Directory, 2005, London and New York, Europa Publications.

Sobhan, Rehman (1989). 'The State and Development of Capitalism: The Third World Perspective', Bharadwaj, K. and Kaviraj, S. (eds), *Perspectives on Capitalism*, New Delhi, Sage Publications.

South Commission (1990). 'The Challenge to the South', New York, Oxford University Press.

Stephens, Gina (2002). 'The Root of the New Consensus: The United States and the Transformation of the G8 System', Kirton, John J. and Takase, J. (eds), *New Directions in Global Political Governance*, England, Ashgate.

Stiglitz, Joseph (2002). *Globalization and its Discontents*, New Delhi, Penguin Books.

Strange, Susan (2008). 'Wake Up, Krasner! The World has Changed', Cameron, Angus et al. (ed.), *International Political Economy*, Vol. I, London, Sage Publications.

Streeten, Paul (1981). 'Development Perspectives', London, Macmillan.

Takase, Junichi (2002). 'The Changing G8 Summit and Japanese Foreign Policy', Kirton, John J. and Takase J. (eds), *New Directions in Global Political Governance*, England, Ashgate.

Taylor, Lance (2002). 'Global Macroeconomic Management', Nayyar, Deepak (ed.), *Governing Globalization, Issues and Institutions*, New Delhi, Oxford Univ. Press.

Taylor, Trevor (1980). 'Power Politics', in Taylor, Trevor (ed.), *Approaches and Theory in International Relations*, London, Longman.

The Economist, 1997-2008, several issues, London (www.economist.com).

\, 2005, London and New York, Europa Publications.

Tinbergen, Jan (1965). *International Economic Integration*, Amsterdam, Elsevier Pub. Co.

Toye, John (1987). *'Dilemmas of Development, Reflections on the Counter-Revolution in Development theory and Policy'*, New York, Basil Blackwell.

UNCTAD, 1997-2002, *World Investment Report*, several issues, New Delhi, India, Bookwell.

UNDP, 1994-2002, *Human Development Report*, New York, Oxford Univ. Press.

United Nations, 1998, 2000, 2001-2002, 2005, Department of World Economic and Social Affairs, *World Economic and Social Survey*, New York.

United Nations, 1999, *World Economic Survey*, New York.

United Nations, Economic and Social Commission for Asia and the Pacific, 2006, *Economic and Social Survey of Asia and the Pacific*, Academic Foundation, New Delhi.

US Department of State, Office of International Information Programs, *US Foreign Policy Agenda*, n.d.

Vital, David, (1972). *The Inequality of States*, Oxford, England, Clarendon Press.

Vora, B. (2003). 'Behind the US' Unilateral War in Iraq, Will Dollar's Hegemony Face a Downfall?', *Mainstream*, April 12.

Wallensteen, P. (2002). *Understanding Conflict Resolution: War, Peace and the Global System*, London, Sage Pub.

Wallerstein, Immanuel (1987). *Historical Capitalism*, UK, Verso.

Watson, Tim (2006). 'An American Empire?', in James, P. and Nairn, T. (eds.), *Globalization and Violence*, Vol. 1, London, Sage Publications.

Weiss, Linda (1997). 'Globalization and the Myth of the Powerless State', *New Left Review*, No. 225, Sept.-Oct.

Whitmeyer, J.M. (1997). 'Mann's Theory of Power – a (Sympathetic) Critique', *The British Journal of Sociology*, 48(2).

Wilken, F. (1982). *The Liberation of Capital*, London, George Allen & Unwin.

Wilkinson, M.D. (1996). 'Lobbying for Fair Trade: Northern NGDOs, The European Community and the GATT Uruguay Round', *Third World Quarterly*, 17(2), June.

Williamson, John (2008). 'The Strange History of the Washington Consensus', in Cameron, Angus et al (ed.), *International Political Economy*, Vol. III, London, Sage Publications.

World Bank, 1993-2002, World Development Report, New York, Oxford University Press.

World Bank, 1998/99, World Development Indicators, Washington D.C., The World Bank

World Bank, 1999-2003, Global Development Finance, Washington D.C., The World Bank.

Zhong, Yang (1996). 'Legitimacy Crisis and Legitimization in China', *Journal of Contemporary Asia*, 26(2).

Zurn, Michael (2001). 'Political systems in the post national constellation: Societal denationalization and multilevel governance', in Rittberger, Volker (ed.), *Global Governance and the United Nations System*, Tokyo, United Nations Univ. Press.

Web sites

http.web.sipri.org/contents/milap/milex/mex_data_index.html
http://meaindia.nic.in/pressbriefing/2004/01/22pb01.htm
http://webscript.princeton.edu/~afp/vol003_iss08/12.shtml
http://www.g20.org/public/index.
http://www.g7.org.
http://www.globalpolicy.org/finance/tables/index.htm
http://www.globalpolicy.org/security/data/vetogph2.htm
http://www.hartford-hwp.com/archives/60/018.htm
http://www.southasiamonitor.org/economy/2004/jun/14eco1.html
http://www.sovereignity.net/p/gov/gganalysis.htm
http://www.un.org/aboutun/charter
http://www.un.org/aboutun/charter/
www.003f.html..newspubse.html../newspubs e.html
www.photius.com dt. 7/7/2000
www.sice.oas.org, May 7th, 2004